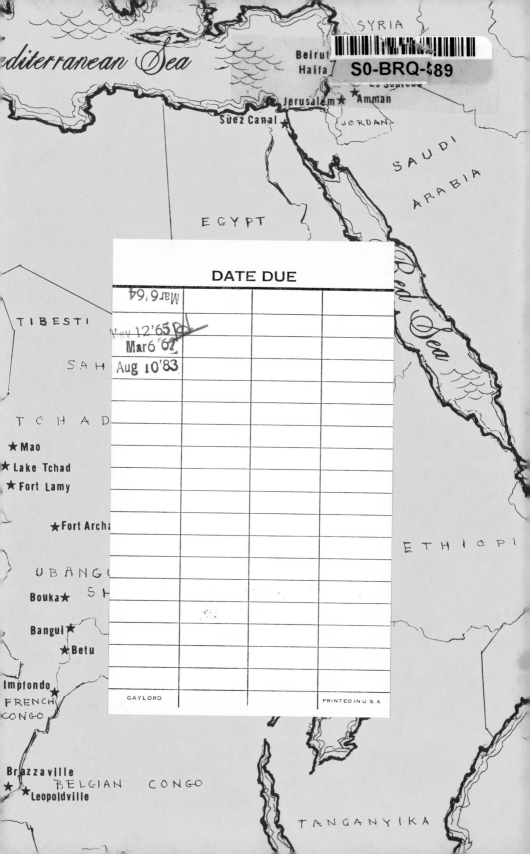

DATE DUE

Mar 6 '64			
May 12 '65			
Mar 6 '67			
Aug 10 '83			
GAYLORD		PRINTED IN U.S.A	

THE
GENERALS
WEAR
CORK HATS

BOOKS BY BEN LUCIEN BURMAN

THE GENERALS WEAR CORK HATS

IT'S A BIG CONTINENT

THE OWL HOOTS TWICE AT CATFISH BEND

THE STREET OF THE LAUGHING CAMEL

IT'S A BIG COUNTRY

SEVEN STARS FOR CATFISH BEND

THE FOUR LIVES OF MUNDY TOLLIVER

HIGH WATER AT CATFISH BEND

CHILDREN OF NOAH

EVERYWHERE I ROAM

ROOSTER CROWS FOR DAY

MIRACLE ON THE CONGO

BIG RIVER TO CROSS

BLOW FOR A LANDING

STEAMBOAT ROUND THE BEND

MISSISSIPPI

BEN LUCIEN BURMAN

THE
GENERALS
WEAR
CORK HATS

☆

*An Amazing Adventure
that Made World History*

Sketches by
ALICE CADDY

TAPLINGER PUBLISHING CO., INC.,
New York

THE Feb. 64
GENERALS
WEAR
CORK HATS... *First Edition*

for FRED FERGUSON

DOUGHTY OLD WARRIOR

WHO AS HE TAKES HIS EASE

in THE NEWSPAPERMAN'S VALHALLA

I HOPE WILL ENJOY

THIS BOOK

CONTENTS

A note for the politically
and historically minded
and any reader
not in a hurry

Despite some kindly urging now and then, I have never been inclined to write my autobiography. A book to me is something that should be put together only when it cries out to be written, for its uniqueness, its entertainment, its information, or some other good reason. I don't feel that my life as a whole is interesting or unusual enough to warrant cutting down a lot of trees to make the necessary paper.

But this part of my life, spent with the Free French and the British in Africa and some of the Arab countries during World War II, is a different matter. It seems to me to have many of the elements of a novel, with a beginning, a middle, and a climactic end.

As a result I have set it down here with much the same feeling and much the same objectivity as though I were writing a work of fiction. I am not a historian. I leave to Churchill and De Gaulle and the generals in the cork hats the putting down of the day-by-day events, the troop movements, the number of tanks destroyed and ammunition dumps exploded. This book is intended for the lay reader, and I hope he will turn its pages with interest.

But for the historically minded, since the narrative involves so many important events of the time and so many individuals still in the public eye, I should state at the outset that every detail so far as I have been able to write it, is absolutely true. There are no imaginary conversations, no conscious exaggerations. As a novelist I was many times tempted to dramatize some extraordi-

INTRODUCTION

nary encounter, to embroider some already bizarre situation. As a conscientious reporter, I have carefully resisted the temptation. I made elaborate notes at the time, and unless my memory has tricked me in some unimportant detail, the account is strictly factual. Where my notes are lacking and my memory is hazy, I take pains to tell the reader so.

I am afraid that some of my many French friends, devout worshipers of General De Gaulle, will be very unhappy about this book, and what I have to say about their hero. De Gaulle is a complex character in a great but complex nation. When I lived with my wife Alice in Paris during the late Twenties and early Thirties, I often remarked to our Parisian intimates that to me the chief difficulty with France politically and economically was that the French Revolution has never been completed. The gulf between the upper and lower classes was so wide, the contempt of some of the rich for the poor so profound, it was impossible for an American to understand. This above all else, in my opinion, created the mentality of Pétain and his associates; it is also the reason that De Gaulle, with his Louis the Fourteenth egotism, can still flourish today. Despite the terrific individualism of its people, to whom I am devoted, France for some of its citizens has still to go through the painful process of becoming a true democracy.

The actions of De Gaulle himself in recent months can have come as no surprise to those who like myself have had an earlier knowledge of his character. I kept

xii

silent about De Gaulle when silence seemed to me necessary to help restore captive France and to help win the
war. After keeping that silence for over twenty years,
I feel it necessary to speak out. De Gaulle's shocking re-
jection of England was a logical development of the
events through which he was created and the later events
detailed in these pages. Despite all his talk of grandeur,
De Gaulle was and is suffering from a terrible inferiority complex. De Gaulle was created by England, nour-
ished by England, sanctified by England. Without
England in the war De Gaulle as we know him today
would never have existed; with English aid withdrawn
De Gaulle would not have lasted ten minutes. For one
of his haughty nature to be a dependent for so many years
must have been desperate humiliation. What a joy at last
to kick his patron in the teeth! On the other hand, Germany, the enemy, was defeated. So Germany could be
treated with condescension.

I wish for the good of the world and humanity that in
a quieter moment he might think back to those black days
when England was his only hope, to which he clung
desperately, as a sailor clings to a life raft after his ship
goes down. The war in Africa during the early days
showed that Britons and Frenchmen can be friends and
work in the closest harmony; there is no basic reason why
they cannot live harmoniously in times of peace.

There is one mystery in the Free French episode I have
never been able to solve to my satisfaction—the bitter
enmity of the American government to the Free French

movement, quite apart from any personal hostility to De Gaulle, its chief. I came on many possibilities. But I have never been certain of the truth. There are two explanations which seem more likely than any of the others. One was that the rich and powerful Vichy lobby had strong social links with the State Department and with men close to President Roosevelt. The other was the possibility, discussed in whispers, of religious influence. Most of my Free French friends were devout Catholics. But they were liberal Catholics, having little support among the reactionary members of the Roman hierarchy. The Catholic world was widely split over the issue, with the reactionaries favoring Vichy, which was frankly advancing the narrower interests of the Church everywhere; the liberals, including even priests in uniform, battled for the Free French. It was the reactionary group whose influence was paramount in Washington. But these are only theories. I doubt if even those who were wielding the influence really know the riddle's answer.

I hope the book will be of some value in another area —helping to understand Africa. There are many who foolishly believe that because certain sections of that vast continent have become sovereign states, and members of the great brotherhood of the United Nations, they can overnight take their place in a cultured, democratic society. Nothing can be farther from the truth. There is a vast difference between the Negro in America who for so many years has been such a vital part of American culture and bred individuals like Ralph Bunche and Langston Hughes, and the black man in numerous areas of

Africa, who as these pages show is only a few moments removed from the stone age. When it is remembered how even in the United States pockets of a culture like the Kentucky Mountaineers or the Cajuns of Louisiana have stubbornly persisted, it is easy to understand the enormous difficulties facing the tiny minority of educated Africans as they labor to bring their fellow black men out of their primeval forests into the age of space.

This volume falls naturally into three parts, the first telling how as a war correspondent I became involved in these strange affairs and became Ambassador In Spite Of Myself; the second giving a glimpse of some of the astonishingly primitive black men through whose territories I passed on the way to the Front; the third relating some fantastic, extracurricular adventures in the Middle East and the hitherto hidden details of certain historic events which I have been compelled by my own judgment to keep secret until now. The Generals Wear Cork Hats of necessity must follow in places the same route taken in my little war book, Miracle On The Congo, published in 1942 and made up chiefly of my dispatches and editorials written after my return. Where the narrative is concerned with the same areas or the same subjects, with a few unavoidable exceptions like De Gaulle's revelations about Pétain, which were of such great importance, I have used different material. Even though the other book has been out of print many years, I have a strong aversion to using the same words twice. If there should be any conflict between the earlier book and this one, The Generals Wear Cork Hats must take precedence. Miracle On

INTRODUCTION

The Congo was published under strict war-time censorship, with names and places and details changed if necessary for security.

There are many to whom I am deeply indebted for this book; merely to put down their names would fill several type-written pages. Suffice it that my heartfelt thanks go to Fritz Dashiell, managing editor and vice president of the *Reader's Digest*, and to Fred Ferguson, president of NEA *Service* (Scripps-Howard) who arranged to publish my stories and thus made the trip possible; to Geoffrey Parsons, chief of the editorial page of the *New York Herald Tribune* and Harry Baehr, his assistant, who published my attacks on American policy in their columns; to Sir Miles Clifford, then British Colonial Secretary in Nigeria, in whose house I became The Man Who Stayed To Dinner; to Air Commodore Buss through whom I wandered into The Thousand And Second Adventure of the Arabian Nights; to the Emir Atrach for his gracious hospitality those two eventful days in the bleak Druse Mountains of Syria; to Colonel and Zuleina Brunschwig, without whom none of this would have happened; to General Sicé and General Leclerc, my patients hosts and friends those troubled days in the sweltering Congo and the blistering Tchad; and to all my other friends, those heroic Free Frenchmen, British, and Australians in Africa and the Middle East, who even in the midst of the degradation and horror of war taught me something of the dignity of man.

BEN LUCIEN BURMAN

I.
AMBASSADOR
WITHOUT
PORTFOLIO

1.
Cloak and Dagger

As far as I am concerned this might be a manuscript found in a bottle.

You know the sort of novel so popular among the fancy-cravated gentlemen and crinoline-clad ladies of the last century which began: "Addressed to Dr. Johann Serviatus A.C.F.R.G.S. care British Museum, London," and then whirled the reader off to an iceberg floating in the Arctic Ocean or perhaps a smoking crater on the planet Venus or Mars.

But the extraordinary part of this particular story is that it actually took place. It is a tale so fantastic, so far removed from the rest of my life that sometimes I begin to have doubts myself. And then I look at the documents on my desk before me and my grim juju and my quiver of poison arrows hanging on the wall, and I know again that it all really happened.

I've started to write the story half a dozen times; and then for the sake of a number of people still alive I put down my pen and closed up my typewriter. But now I feel I shouldn't delay any longer. If I don't tell what happened it will never be written and certain obscure events will remain a mystery.

It all started with a fish, or rather two fishermen. I was living in Hollywood writing a film about the South for Paramount Pictures, when France surrendered to the invading Germans. The French collapse, made final at Vichy, shook the world like a cosmic explosion. It was

3

an even more devastating shock to my personal cosmos. I had been hit by a German shell at Soissons in the Second Battle of The Marne during the First World War, and as a result had spent a long time flat on my back in Army hospitals. I had learned from my own grueling experience the utter stupidity and wastefulness of war.

I disliked Hitler and Mussolini even more than most of my acquaintances because these two figures, who in a rational world would have remained only talking scarecrows with cracked and ridiculous voices, became twin Princes Of Death who made war once more the reigning fashion. Since that melancholy September of 1939 when World War the Second began, I had been attempting to enlist in either the British or the French Army. Because of my earlier encounter with that shell on the placid Marne I had been consistently refused.

With the French armistice that somber June of 1941, overnight the war had become a lunatic's frenzied nightmare. France, the undefeatable, was lost. Britain, though managing to rescue most of her troops in the Miracle of Dunkirk, was now left alone to face a German army that seemed able to sweep across the world at will, as though its soldiers were not men, but robots created in the grotesque brain of a writer of incredible science fiction. Marshal Pétain, hero of the first Great War, who had become head of the Vichy government, was a riddle to America and the world. Was he a heroic old man, taking the post only to lessen his country's agony, or was he simply a traitor?

4

I finished my film for Paramount not long after the Vichy surrender, and coming to New York, met my old friend Dick Mealand, the Paramount editor. Dick chanced to tell me how he went fishing every Sunday with a certain Roger Brunschwig, a famous French manufacturer of artistic textiles who was among the leaders of a shadowy movement in America to deny Pétain and Vichy, and to help Frenchmen fight the Germans. He arranged for me to meet his fishing companion next day. I found Roger Brunschwig in his office, warm, delightful. I had heard vague rumors of Frenchmen who were gathering in some unknown, mysterious region of Africa to resist the French armistice. I asked if there was any way I could manage to visit these rebels and perhaps in this far off land learn the truth about Pétain and his Men Of Vichy.

The Frenchman smiled cryptically. "I am afraid it is quite impossible," he said.

He saw my disappointment and went on to explain. "Our movement is a conspiracy. It means death if any of us are caught. Almost all of us have families in occupied France, who share these dangers. To admit an outsider, however enthusiastic, to a knowledge of our secrets is a risk we dare not take."

I saw him several times afterward, always with the same result. I was ready to give up in despair. And then began the first of a long series of coincidences so capricious, so bizarre that if I used them in a novel I would properly be condemned by my fellows as unworthy of inclusion in good writers' society. I was a confirmed fatalist before these coincidences began; I must certainly have become one by the time they ended. What good is there in intricate planning, when after everything is arranged to the last detail, fate suddenly shuts the door or drops the curtain, only an instant later to open another unseen entrance or to raise a hidden veil? It is little wonder that men are gamblers. Life is fuller of hazards than any game of chance. If that airplane flying me out of Fort Lamy to Cairo had dropped another thousand feet—

One afternoon I had another baffling conversation with Roger Brunschwig. That night he happened to mention my name to his wife. My far-sighted guardian angel must have plotted years before that Roger fall in love and marry a charming American girl from Davenport, Iowa, on the banks of the muddy Mississippi, the river to which in my younger days I had devoted my writing life. That same astute angel surely arranged that this American girl should like my books. Enthusiastically Zuleina Brunschwig set about persuading her husband that with my writing I could help the conspiracy. I was now to learn the truth of that ancient proverb—never underestimate the power of a woman.

I had heard hazy stories of a certain obscure general named De Gaulle who had stubbornly stood out against the surrender, and had been brought to London by Churchill. Within a few days word came from this unknown officer, now the head of the French resistance movement in London that I could make the trip, and thus become the first writer to visit the rebels in their African stronghold, the far-off French Congo.

This was the signal for which I had been waiting, and securing assignments from the *Reader's Digest* and NEA *Service* of the Scripps-Howard organization as a war correspondent, I set about making my preparations for departure.

My artist wife, Alice, to whom I had for many years been devoted, and from whom I had never been separated for more than a few days, asked to be allowed to come along. It was, I knew, a trip that would entail great hardship for many months and considerable danger. This was run-of-the-mine to one like myself, who had been thoroughly involved in one war, and after that been a newspaper reporter. But I hesitated to expose Alice, who was of a delicate physique and the exact opposite of the usual lady explorer, to such hazards. She insisted, however, and I at last yielded. My editors gave her an assignment as an official war artist. The selection of the articles I would take in my limited suitcases, before a simple matter, now became incredibly complicated.

The first important difficulties had thus been resolved. Now I was faced with another problem that for a time seemed beyond solution.

Even in peacetime the French Congo and the other parts of French Equatorial Africa where the rebels were gathering, because of their vast jungles and deserts, were probably the most inaccessible regions in the whole Gallic empire. I quickly discovered that cut off from the mother country by the rebellion, it was now probably one of the most isolated regions in the world.

No traveler since the Vichy armistice had journeyed there from America; no one, not even Roger Brunschwig, could give me a shred of information. I looked at the map of Africa and studied the area where we would be journeying. It appeared almost as unexplored, as desolate as when Stanley searched in the steaming forests, hoping to find some faint trace of the lost Dr. Livingstone.

I will pass over the numerous false starts, the wearying disappointments in the weeks that followed while I investigated every known means of travel. But at last one bitter morning in the winter of 1941 we set out in a taxicab toward La Guardia Airport, bound for Lisbon, and I hoped, Africa and the war. A heavy snow had fallen, covering the sidewalks with parallel downy carpets, still untouched by the soot and grime which would defile them later. We drove along the streets piled high near the curbs with snow thrown there by the mechanical sweepers, like endless ranges of miniature white mountains. Soon we arrived at the airplane dock where a graceful Pan American Clipper lay moored in the ice-fringed water.

We took our seats and I patted my thick brown envelope filled with secret documents to make sure it was still safe inside my coat pocket. I realized more than ever,

as Roger Brunschwig had told me, that it was a dangerous matter, a conspiracy. A cigarette paper dropped in
the wrong hotel lobby, a careless word spoken in the
wrong café could mean a hundred lives. At Lisbon, the
end of the first lap of this journey that was to lead I
knew not where, I was to present one of the documents
in this envelope to a certain mysterious individual whom
I will call for lack of a better designation Monsieur X,
the chief conspirator in the Portuguese capital, which
because of its strategic location had become the spies'
mother-of-pearl paradise.

I have forgotten the exact details—for obvious reasons I kept no notes here—but as I remember, to ferret
out this Monsieur X was a highly complicated procedure.
It was all very cloak and daggery—the sort of thing
where one goes to a certain furniture store and asks to
look at a certain piece of antique furniture, and there is
directed to a phonograph shop, where the inquirer asks
the clerk to play a certain unusual record, never asked
for by the casual music lover; if his credentials are found
satisfactory, he is then led to the master, Monsieur X
himself.

This was a new experience, being involved in a plot
against a government. I felt as if I were playing the part
of the hero in a mystery melodrama. I would not have
been much surprised to see flashing on a screen in the
airplane cabin the usual "Directed By" and "Cast of
Characters."

The great propellors of the clipper began to whir and

the plane rose heavily into the sky. Against the roofs of the city, sometimes white with snow, sometimes black where it had drifted away and exposed the metal or tar, the towers of New York rose like ivory castles set on a gigantic chessboard.

Since war's ultimate aim is death, there is apt to be at the beginning of such a journey an instant of wondering if you are destined to be among the lucky ones who will come back. Watching Alice sitting quietly by the window, I was swept by a feeling of deep guilt. If anything happened to her on this hazardous expedition, unsuited for a woman, the blame would be only mine. But I am not one given to morbid reflection. The decision had been made, right or wrong; it was now my duty to devote myself to the task that lay ahead, and try to find out the truth.

The plane settled down to a steady droning above a somber ocean. I began to explore the luxurious cabin and its occupants. We were perhaps twenty-five passengers, almost all with diplomatic credentials, for the Clipper flights were few and no one could obtain a seat without a high priority.

I studied the varied faces as I walked down the aisle, the counselors of foreign embassies, solemn, tired men, weary of the chaotic world which defied their strained attempts at wisdom; the State Department couriers, carrying briefcases full of mysterious documents, nervous figures with tight-locked lips who reminded me of poodles carrying their ladies' handbags, always with an anxious look in their eyes as if they might open their mouths and thus let the handbags and the secrets fall.

Two American diplomats sat near me, Averill Harriman, named Lend-Lease Administrator to the Allies as the result of a bill just passed by Congress, and Anthony Biddle, better known as Tony, Ambassador To The Invaded Countries. I chatted with Mr. Harriman awhile as men chatted in those days, about the war and international politics, then joined Tony Biddle, sitting across the aisle. It is curious how sometimes an impression can be formed from an account in the press that must be thoroughly erased on meeting the reality. I had always thought of Tony Biddle as the perfect Philadelphia playboy. I found him in actuality quite the contrary, informed, thoughtful, with a leavening sense of humor. We talked pleasantly. And then came another of those strange coincidences that in a split second can completely alter a plan or change a life.

I am not sure this one was arranged by my guardian angel. Sometimes I think in the light of what happened that it may have been planned by a wandering devil while my usually alert guardian angel was asleep. Our plane came down at Bermuda to refuel. While a flood of gasoline was being pumped into the tanks word came of a violent storm sweeping the sea between us and the Azores, our next stop. Instead of continuing our flight, in those days of flying boats that could not soar into the stratosphere, we were compelled to stay in Bermuda a full day and a night. Somehow it happened that much of that time I spent talking with Tony Biddle.

Our talk passed from the casual to the serious. I told him of my intended visit to the French rebels in Africa. He in turn informed me that the United States had no representative in this area. He reflected a moment, then went on to say that as Ambassador To The Invaded Countries the French collapse was his gravest concern. Would I study the African situation after my arrival and cable what I thought to him in London? It would, he added, be of vital importance; he would immediately pass on my impressions and opinions to Secretary of State Hull and the White House in Washington. He did not need to add one important fact which I already knew: the State Department policy was pro-Pétain and pro-Vichy.

Word came next morning that the storm had ended. The plane set off with the sky and ocean both an iridescent blue instead of the sickly gray of the day previous. I, too, had changed overnight. I felt a little like those African gorillas I expected soon to be seeing, who legend said, pounded their chests as they swelled with hairy pride. I was now not only a character in a mystery melodrama. I was by proxy a U.S. Ambassador—without portfolio and without expense account. I blessed the story I had just written for Paramount which had given me a cheerful balance in the bank.

12

A long day passed and a long night. I strolled up toward the cockpit, stumbling over Averill Harriman's long, outstretched legs as he dozed fitfully in his seat. Not far away the State Department couriers were dozing as well, again like nervous poodles, watchful of the briefcases on their laps, even in their sleep. I joined the pilot, and sat watching the stars twinkling about me, like bits of mica set around the inside of a black pottery bowl.

Funchal showed ahead, then Lisbon and the wide Tagus, black with smoking river craft. I arranged—I had better not say in what manner even now—to slip my envelope of secret papers past the Portuguese guards; I had been cautioned that some of these officials were in the pay of German agents. We stepped out of the plane and saw a newspaper associate, a dry, cynical journalist of the old hard-bitten breed, waiting to meet us on the dock. As we boarded a taxi, the plot of the melodrama thickened.

"Be careful in your hotel," he warned, as he toyed with a cigarette lighter. "Don't leave any papers anywhere. Spying is big business here. So many escudos for a copy of a letter arriving at an embassy; so many escudos for the time of a convoy coming in or going out. Fixed rates, too, so the prices won't be knocked down by competition. It wouldn't surprise me if there's a spies' union."

We drove through the streets, where barefoot women

13

with huge trays of fish on their heads were crying their wares, and arriving at our hotel, dumped our bags, and went off to a nearby restaurant for dinner. The tables were crowded with men and women from every country in Europe. Here was a family of refugees, a dignified, white-haired old man and his courtly wife and polite children, all speaking a language which I could not understand; the faces of the old people were marked deep with the lines that came from constant fear of the fatal knock in the middle of the night. Here were gay-mustachioed Italian officers, toasting Mussolini in expensive wine, and fat Nazi storm-troopers with the Hitler cross on their sleeves, talking in loud voices and gorging mountains of meat and fish and foaming cataracts of beer.

We returned to our hotel. My cynical newspaper colleague was right. Our suitcases had all been opened and the contents examined in our absence, then not too skilfully replaced with the hope of leaving no sign. Though if the fee for the examiner was more than the price of a cheap Portuguese drink, he would have been much overpaid. Every important paper I possessed was in my coat pocket, safely tucked away in that thick brown envelope.

In the morning I hurried off to the British Embassy to present the first of my letters. I mentioned to the quiet-spoken English official into whose quarters I had been ushered that later I must find the mysterious Monsieur X.

"Perhaps I can save you a bit of trouble," he remarked. "Monsieur X has moved to our Embassy. Just one flight up those stairs."

I was gravely disappointed. It would have been far more exciting to visit the furniture store and the music shop and ask for the period chair and the record of which no ordinary customer had ever heard. I felt aggrieved that Monsieur X had not delayed his moving until my arrival. This was no secret mission, merely to mount a flight of stairs.

I was further disappointed for a moment when I found Monsieur X in his office, a mild looking little man with more the air of a bank clerk receiving a small deposit in a French provincial town than one whose daily routine was plots and counterplots, and stern matters of life and death.

But when he spoke his words quickly belied his appearance. They were charged with excitement and mystery. "We are putting you and your wife on a Portuguese ship," he declared. "The Lourenço Marques. She will land you at San Antonio Do Zaire, a village in Portuguese Africa you will not find on your map, at the mouth of the Congo. We are rebels and the Portuguese will not bring their boats into our waters. From San Antonio Do Zaire you will make your way to Brazzaville, the capital of French Equatorial Africa. That is the center where our men are now gathering."

An English secretary entered bearing a letter. He signed it and passed it to me across his desk. "On the

15

Lourenço Marques there will be a lady with her daughter. I cannot tell even you who she is, for secrecy is vital. But I will tell her you are aboard; in case of emergency she will reveal her identity. . . . Your boat leaves tomorrow at four."

It was with something of dismay that I heard the time of our departure. I had expected at least several days to make our preparations. My hard-bitten, pessimistic newspaper colleague had told me it would take weeks to complete the exit visas and the other elaborate formalities before we could leave Lisbon. Now we had only a few hours.

Breathlessly, with Ambassador Biddle's help, we dashed from embassy to embassy securing in minutes visas that ordinarily might take a month; frantically we raced about, buying cork helmets and white tropicals and vast quantities of quinine, and the usual romantic picture-book equipment I had read was needed by every African adventurer. At the end of the day only a fraction of our tasks were accomplished, and perhaps half of the consular and embassy rubber stamps were on the proper pages of our passports. We stayed up all night rearranging our baggage, and shortly after dawn, when the porters of the first stores to open were sweeping the sidewalks with enormous brooms, started on our hectic rounds again. So frenzied was our pace, so unlike the usual leisurely Lisbon ways, that we broke down three of the local, woebegone taxis. I had run out of cash now, and the taxi bills had mounted.

"I'll pay you at the dock this afternoon at four!" I shouted to each driver I was abandoning, and leaped into another cab for a new giddy scramble.

At ten minutes of four we finished the final errand. But we were still miles away from the dock. A New York friend had given me a casual letter to a banker acquaintance in Lisbon. From my newspaper colleague I had learned the banker was a director of the steamship line on which we were sailing. Frantically I called him on the telephone; he said he would try to hold the boat. Madly we dashed through the teeming streets, again and again avoiding a collision with a horse pulling a dilapidated cart full of wine casks or a solemn, silvery moustached old man transporting a mountain of bundles on a bicycle. We neared the harbor and I saw the three taxicabs I had hired in the morning, waiting like birds of prey before a gloomy warehouse. They saw us at the same instant, and whirling into line behind, joined in our fevered race. We reached the water's edge and my heart sank. The quay was empty. Long lines of stevedores were issuing like ants from the dock gates, their work of preparing the boat for departure finished. I looked at my watch. It was fifteen minutes after four.

I saw the ship, moving slowly down the bay, out toward the Atlantic. I paid off the taxi men and watched in despair. Suddenly a tug swung up to the dock before us. A Portuguese sailor leaped ashore, gesticulating wildly.

"Come aboard, Senhor!" he shouted.

In a moment we were scudding down the choppy harbor. I looked across the water again. The banker had done his work well. The Lourenço Marques had stopped and was awaiting our arrival. The stretch of white-capped water between our tug and the ship rapidly grew smaller. We drew alongside and bobbing violently, watched while the deckhands above lowered a narrow ship's ladder. We climbed it and stepped aboard the deck where a trim Portuguese officer was standing. Behind him were half a dozen passengers, grumbling at the delay.

"This way, Senhor," said the officer.

It was a fit beginning for a voyage into the unknown.

I found her a pleasant ship, the Lourenço Marques, as we went down to dinner, her passengers mostly government administrators and young army officers and their wives bound for Angola and Mozambique and Goa. I looked about the dining room with curiosity, trying to decide which of the five or six women with daughters sitting at the tables was the mysterious lady of Monsieur X. I continued my guessing game for several days, and decided for no good reason, that the likeliest was a smartly groomed woman who as I remember claimed Poland as her home, and who we will call here Madame Radowski—I have forgotten her exact name. She had with her a quiet-spoken daughter perhaps sixteen who vaguely reminded me of a girl I had known in High School.

The voyage proceeded uneventfully as the boat moved steadily southward. Past Madeira we sailed, and the Canaries, with the white peak of Tenerife suspended in the sky above the clouds like a ghost mountain in a Japanese painting. Often we were traveling close to the African shore. With field glasses I could see a stretch of silvery beach and palm trees and sometimes a tiny village or a town. We were on the direct track of the boats sailing from England to South Africa, and German U-boats were prowling constantly around us.

Occasionally in the distance we would see a great convoy, a score of merchant ships with destroyers patrolling back and forth alongside, like restless watch dogs guarding a flock of sheep. Sometimes at night a blacked-out freighter, traveling swiftly and alone, would pass our bow like a furtive ghost, seeking to escape from phantom pursuers. The radio room of our boat, in peacetime always a busy, cheerful place, alive with the chattering of a hundred garrulous craft steaming somewhere on the nearby ocean, was silent, deserted. The frightened ships had lost their voices.

But most of the time I was tempted to forget the war-torn world outside. The weather was glorious; the Lourenço Marques was a neutral ship, with little fear of Nazi submarines. From any outward sign we might have been on a tropical cruise, our only concern how many varieties of Portuguese hors d'oeuvres we would have for lunch, or who would win the ship's pool when the purser posted the day's run on the bulletin board in the cabin. Each night after dinner an amateurish orchestra played American jazz while the pretty Portuguese wives danced with their officer husbands. One evening there was a *jantar American*, whatever strange affair a *jantar* might be; I being an American, achieved one of my childhood ambitions and was permitted to play the drums. I played till I was weary, deciding in my next incarnation that I would be the kettle drummer in a symphony orchestra. I still haven't solved the riddle of *jantar*.

But the day following this particularly gay dance any drift toward a lotus-eater's existence, any tendency to ignore the war, ended with a shock. It was no longer a secret where I was heading, for on coming aboard the boat it had been necessary to tell the purser our destination; for the first time I now heard the area being called Free French Africa. What a ship's purser hears is known at once from the sailor in the crow's nest to the lowliest stoker shoveling coal in the ship's bottom. Since the purpose of my trip was now common property, I had no hesitation in discussing it with some of those men and women who had been in nearby colonies, thinking I might in this way gain some useful information.

I was talking after dinner in this fashion with a group of passengers on the promenade deck, when I happened to remark that I was going to send a telegram to the Free French authorities in Brazzaville, advising them that we would soon be arriving. As I spoke I noticed that Madame

Radowski, the Polish lady with the quiet daughter, turned white as the nearby lifeboat shining in the moonlight.

A moment later she drew me aside, and spoke in a voice taut with anxiety, "Monsieur, I beg you. Do not send that telegram."

I looked at her in astonishment. It was an odd request to come from a woman to whom I had spoken casually perhaps half a dozen times on the voyage.

I answered, I am afraid, somewhat coldly, "It is an important telegram, Madame. I must ask you why."

I noticed then that her hands like her cheeks were bloodless. "You are, are you not the gentleman Monsieur X spoke to me about in Lisbon?"

"I am that person, Madame."

She tugged nervously at her handkerchief, as though trying to make a decision. "You are sending your telegram, are you not, to General De Larminat, the High Commissioner of Free French Africa?"

"Yes, Madame."

She grew hesitant again. "My name is not Radowski. I am not Polish. I am a Frenchwoman, traveling on a false passport. I am Madame De Larminat."

A sailor approached to fasten down a tarpaulin covering the lifeboat. She waited until he had moved away. "For months I was in occupied France, trying to escape with my daughter from the Vichy government and the Gestapo. After many attempts I succeeded, as you see.

Because of my husband's importance, the Germans are furious. I am a valuable hostage and they have put a high price on my head. They would use any means to bring me back."

She glanced off toward the starry horizon where during the day, through the field glasses, I had noticed new stretches of silvery beaches and waving palms. "I have just sent a radio in code to my husband in Brazzaville. It was a telegram that could not be avoided. We are only a few miles from Dakar, where, alas, the Vichy governor is very powerful. His men are watching the signals from every ship so that they may give their information to the Germans. No one ever sends a telegram from a ship passing here to Brazzaville. If you send yours that will make two telegrams. The governor is likely to become suspicious, and order out a destroyer to take us both away."

I did not send the telegram.

2

I Wear a Cork Hat

Past the steaming forests of Sierra Leone and the Gold Coast and Nigeria we voyaged, into the torrid Gulf of Guinea. We were taking quinine regularly now, for this was the land of the mosquitoes that brought blackwater fever and the tsetse flies that infected the blood with the deadly sleeping sickness; this was the sinister area known as the white man's tomb. Often I would stand watching the matted jungles that marked the shore, and think of the great book with a padded binding given me when I was a small boy for my birthday. It was a volume of Stanley's Travels In Africa. On the cover was a picture in grisly colors of a giant python crushing a struggling elephant in its coils.

We crossed the Equator, and packed our belongings. We were nearing our goal. Suddenly, though no land was visible, the blue of the sea became a murky yellow, like the muddy mouth of the Mississippi. These were the waters of the Congo, bringing down the soil of half a continent, and reaching out with grimy fingers many miles beyond the shore. Soon a hazy green thread showed far away where the water met the sky. The Lourenço Marques came to a stop, and dropped its anchor. A launch, flying the Portuguese flag, came speeding toward us. We descended a ladder with half a dozen Belgians bound for Matadi up the river, and climbing aboard, moved off toward the green thread in the distance. I turned to watch as the Lourenço Marques raised her

25

anchor. She swung about, and giving a melancholy blast of her whistle, as though in farewell, disappeared into the horizon. Our last link with civilization was broken.

The green thread widened, becoming a tangled mangrove swamp over which a vulture was flying funereally. A native village became visible, set close to the water. We tied up before it and stepped onto the spongy bank. It was a perfect setting for my book with the padded cover and every fervid African romance I had read in my childhood. A dozen huts like enormous square beehives stood a short distance apart, bordered by palms and banana trees. Before them, Negro women in gaudy-patterned robes were walking, gracefully balancing bundles of wood and jars of water on their heads. Here and there half-naked black men were sitting, smoking pipes or eating the food the women brought them in earthen bowls, and talking in voices liquid as honey. Some swarthy white children studied us gravely, each wearing huge brass earrings and carrying a bright green parrot on an arm. In the dark forest beyond tom-toms beat monotonously.

"It's not true," I said to Alice. "This is a Cecil B. De Mille production."

We had arrived at San Antonio Do Zaire, in the colony of Cabinda, the first and last outpost of the tsetse-ridden Congo. As I had been told in Lisbon, the Portuguese steamship company wanted no diplomatic complications with French rebels. If any foolish traveler wished to visit the conspirators' territory, the captain dropped him at this desolate settlement, unfit to dock a large rowboat, and let him take the consequences of his folly.

A sad-faced Portuguese and his wife led us off to a bleak frame building resembling a large lean-to, wide open at both ends.

"Will you take us to the hotel, Senhor?" I asked.

He turned to me in reproach. "This is the hotel, Senhor."

I looked again and saw a few dingy cots set about the broken floor. We selected the two seeming less dilapidated than the others, while some black boys carried in our valises.

Night fell with tropical swiftness. By the light of a smoky kerosene lamp we ate some tasteless meat and soggy bananas, then carrying a flickering candle made our way to the lean-to. We undressed and crawled beneath the musty mosquito nets draped over our cots. I stretched my hand under the netting to bring the candle flickering on a stand nearer to the bed in case we would need it in the night. I blew it out.

It was as though the action were the signal given by a stage director for a well-rehearsed play to begin. From all sides of us there came the thousand eerie voices of Africa. Strange insects chanted weirdly in the trees with a noise like drums or rushing water, and frogs broke into a frenzied croaking like bells or blacksmiths pounding on

27

great anvils. Night birds called with sounds like the pop-
ping of corks in wine bottles or the trotting of horses
over stones. Some animal in the distance howled dismally
like a child in pain; there followed a demoniac laugh that
I recognized from a stay in the Sahara many years before
—the blood-curdling voice of the hyena. From another
quarter of the blackness there came a shrill cry of rage
followed by a wail of agony, and then a final scream of
triumph as some unwary animal became the prey of a
prowling enemy in the bitter, never-ending war that is
the jungle.

Alice and I tried to sleep, but found it impossible.
Suddenly there was a curious noise of something moving
cautiously across the floor, and the musty smell of a
sweating animal. Gingerly in the darkness I raised the
mosquito net and lit the candle, to see a shadowy form
resembling a hyena scurrying off toward the forest. I
blew out the candle again. New patterings of animal feet
followed. In the obscurity I could vaguely distinguish
some huge kind of rat, then a trio of jackals, probably
seeking to steal a native chicken. Our lodging was obviously a favorite highway, an animal African turnpike.
Wearily I blew out the candle again.

There came a more sinister sound, now a curious rustle,
now an eerie crackling as though a huge snake were
crawling under my cot. In alarm this time I relit the
candle. On the floor near my head an army of ants was

struggling with a black beetle, big as a saucer, trying to pull it down through a gaping crack in the boards. I rescued the forlorn creature from its tormentors and with a palm frond brushed them outside. I crawled back into bed, hoping for a little rest.

My hope was vain. All night Alice and I lay there while the animals continued to move past in restless procession. I was dozing off at last into a hazy dream, when I was roused by a flash of lightning, followed by a volcanic clap of thunder. New blinding flashes came in quick succession, and new cannonades of thunder. The wind began to howl like a thousand terrified animals in the forest, suddenly gone insane; by the glare of the lightning I could see the trees swaying like dancing savages drunk with native wine. A fierce rain beat upon our sorry shelter. A hundred miniature Niagaras began to pour down upon us from great holes in the roof. In an instant our bedclothes were soggy sponges. We climbed out, soaked to the skin. The cots quickly became sodden pools of water. I tried to light the candle again. The wind was too violent and instantly snuffed it out. We gave up at last, and resigning ourselves to whatever fate might offer, sat down in broken chairs, and waited dismally for the dawn.

It was perhaps four o'clock, and I was once more in that queer state halfway between waking and sleeping, when I jumped up from my chair in fright. A giant

figure appeared at one end of the building, framed
vividly by the continuous flashes of lightning. Enormous
brass earrings swung under his ragged black hair; with
his swarthy face he seemed the ghost of some slave-
trading pirate cruising along the African coast to carry
us off into cruel captivity. In his hand he was carrying a
sputtering lantern.

"Awaken, Senhor," he rumbled. "It is time to start for
Matadi."

We threw on our clothes while he waited outside, then
followed him through the rainy blackness to a tiny dock.
A launch was moored alongside; even in the darkness I
could see the vessel was in the last stages of decay. The
Belgians from the Lourenço Marques were already there,
awaiting our arrival. The Pirate gave some commands to
the silent Negro who formed his crew. The boat set off
up the black water.

It began to grow light. The rain slackened, then ceased
altogether. Through the faint mist lying over the water
I could see that we were traveling close to a tangled wall
of vegetation, like a continuous green waterfall. We
were traveling along the edge of an immense forest,
going up the Congo.

The Pirate, a jovial buccaneer in the daylight, began
to prepare breakfast on a rusty iron stove hanging dan-
gerously in the bow. The crisp smell of frying bacon
drifted pleasantly to our nostrils. The sun came out, and
the last traces of the storm vanished.

Our spirits quickly brightened, and I watched the shore in fascination. This was the Africa I had dreamed of, tangled, sullen, yet full of beauty and wonder. Graceful birds with legs long and thin as the reeds among which they were wading appeared everywhere in front of the green forest wall, while smaller birds of many colors flew above them in jeweled flashes. Giant crocodiles crawled torpidly over the snaky roots stretching out from the trees, pretending not to see the monkeys high above leaping and chattering safely in the branches.

The rickety boat chugged laboriously up the river, rocking in the muddy swells. Now and then the feeble motor would cough unhappily and come to a stop. The pirate would curse under his breath, and leaving his cooking, tinker with the engine. When it coughed weakly again, and the propellor renewed its erratic churning, he would beam upon us with the air of a proud parent who has just accomplished some marvel at a family picnic. A moment later he would return to the battered stove.

Some odd-shaped flies darted out from the steaming bushes on shore toward us.

The pirate hurried over and struck at the insects with a folded newspaper. "Do not let them bite, Senhor. They have the touch of death. They are the tsetses."

We needed no second warning. Our slapping hands became a rhythmic accompaniment to the throbbing of the engine.

The Pirate brought us breakfast. We became cheerful now, and laughed over the trials of the previous night.

All day we traveled, with the crocodiles so inert, so motionless they seemed to be ugly masses of mud thrown out on the bank by some untidy sculptor. Still no trace of the opposite shore was visible. This was an immense river, the Congo, one of the largest in the world.

As the hours passed the sun grew hotter, reflected from the painted deck as though it were a metal sheet that formed the bottom of a broiler. We seemed like dressed chickens, turning on the spit. There was a scrap of ragged awning over part of the deck, dating back to some former day of glory. We moved in a circle around it, like mechanical figures bound by some odd magnetism, following its shadow.

Late in the afternoon a sudden thundercloud swept across the fiery sky. River and shore were plunged into inky blackness. A fierce storm struck us, worse than that we had experienced in the night. The thunder boomed with a violence unlike any I had ever heard; it was as though each thunderclap were inside us, exploding in our bones. The Pirate lit a cheap oil lamp and hung it from the frail mast in the center of the boat.

He grinned at us amiably. "It is a beautiful lamp, senhores," he said. "I have bought it in Luanda, the capital of Angola. It has cost many escudos."

Despite the thunder and lightning there had been no

wind since morning. The squall arrived now, howling like a hurricane. The decrepit craft began to rock giddily.

"Do not be afraid, senhores," said the Pirate. "It is a beautiful boat. The best boat on the Congo."

He steered it toward shore to tie up for safety in a nearby cove. Suddenly the laboring engine began a convulsive sputtering, as though someone were setting off a dozen packs of firecrackers, then gave an asthmatic gasp and grew silent. The boat began to flounder giddily from side to side, seeming at each instant on the verge of overturning. The pirate lashed the wheel and began to tinker desperately with the spark-plugs once more.

A small boy belonging to one of the Belgians chose this moment to climb the mast and start playing with the swaying lamp. With difficulty we pulled him down, just as he was about to jerk it free, an act which would undoubtedly have set both himself and the boat on fire.

The Pirate, clinging to a stanchion, went on feverishly struggling with the motor. With relief at last I heard the familiar drunken hiccup that meant it was about to start. The Pirate steered the vessel into quieter water and moored it to a tree.

For a long time we lay there, tossing sluggishly while the forest world about us seemed to dissolve in a greenish conflagration.

When the storm ended it was night. The moon emerged from the retreating clouds and shone with a

33

cool, peaceful light over the black water. I had learned my first lesson. Equatorial Africa was a never-ending cycle; intense heat, fierce storm, great calm, intense heat, followed by a fierce storm again.

We reached Matadi at last, bustling port of the Belgian Congo, and after a few hours in a hotel boarded an absurd little caricature of a train consisting of half a dozen toy freight cars, and a single toy car jammed to the windows with black passengers. With noisy farewells from the crowd of Negro men and women standing on the platform and an excited hooting of whistles, we rolled out into the countryside. Jerkily the train rattled on, while an elderly Negro wearing a peaked cap squeezed his way through the packed car, gravely collecting fares from the sometimes grinning, sometimes frightened riders. Soldiers carrying rifles moved back and forth importantly, their black skins, like ebony mirrors, contrasting sharply with their gay-colored uniforms. At each stop a crowd of natives would swarm aboard, carrying huge bundles on their heads, the burden occasionally a quartet of chickens or a grunting pig. The rails cut through a dense forest now, so close the windows often brushed the branches. Every moment I expected to see a leopard or an elephant.

The train grew more and more crowded. Negro women in beautiful printed robes sat on bundles in the aisles, with sleeping black babies tied to their waists;

black men stood precariously on the jolting steps outside, clinging to the handrails, and seeming liable at any instant to be decapitated by the trunk of a passing tree. A rooster hidden somewhere under a mound of boxes crowed majestically. A dog nearby barked in angry defiance. There came the sound of a scuffle between fowl and animal, then a wild flapping of wings and a yelp of pain as the battle ended. The tooting of the whistle became continuous. I wondered how the engineer could keep up enough steam.

Native huts began to appear along the track, closer and closer together, then gray factory sheds and warehouses. We were nearing a city. With a shrill squealing of brakes and a triumphant screech of the whistle the train pulled into a railroad station. We had arrived at Kinshasa, better known as Leopoldville, chief city of the Belgian Congo and all Central Africa.

We descended from the train, while a trail of sweating porters followed with our many valises. A stout, ruddy-faced Frenchman was waiting alongside, clad in immaculate white cork hat and white tropicals. He came forward inquiringly.

"Monsieur and Madame Burman?" he asked.

"Yes, Monsieur."

He faced me with solemnity. "I am the representative of General De Gaulle in Leopoldville. In the name of Free France and of General De Gaulle I welcome you to Free French Africa."

35

He reached out his hand.

The trip had been so long, so arduous, and in his white shirt and shorts he was so much the perfect African explorer, it was difficult to keep from saying, "Dr. Livingstone, I presume."

3.
War Is a Melodrama

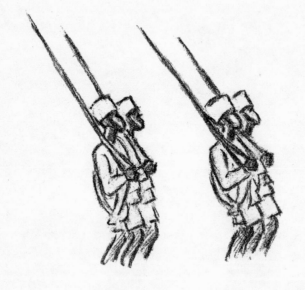

A striking figure in trim military uniform came forward now, a French Apollo. "I am Lieutenant Laurelle," he said in flawless English. "Aide to General De Larminat, the High Commissioner. I will take you across to Brazzaville. I'm afraid you won't find it New York."

We drove down to the banks of the Congo where a little ferry was waiting. The river was three miles wide here, the great Stanley Pool, named for the explorer who had first seen it on his travels many years before. We crossed it swiftly. The boat touched the Brazzaville shore. A khaki-helmeted French officer was waiting with an automobile, a jolly, electric individual whose ruddy skin seemed to have been dried too long in the African sun.

"Major Clapot," said Lieutenant Laurelle, presenting the newcomer. "He'll see that there's a roof over your head."

We drove through the town, a drowsy little settlement typical of the French tropics, a Catholic church, a bank, a mission, a few European houses for the white administrators, and beyond these the straw and adobe huts of the natives. Towering palms grew everywhere, and enormous trees I thought might be baobobs, with spreading trunks seeming wide as a house. Black women in brilliant colored Japanese prints walked along the road, carrying mounds of vegetables or jars of water on their heads, like slaves in an ancient Egyptian painting. Past them helmeted white men dashed about in the Brazzaville

39

taxi, the pous-pous, a vehicle much like the Chinese rickshaw of Hong Kong and Shanghai, only here the motive power was a half-naked Negro of glistening ebony.

Our car drew up before a stately Colonial house with wide verandas, set on the banks of the Congo.

The jovial Major Clapot led the way inside. "This is General De Gaulle's house," he announced. "But in his absence we use it as a guest house. This is to be your home."

He added that the General was too busy in London to come to Brazzaville for many months; we need have no worry about being disturbed.

The two officers left and we hastened to inspect our newly acquired mansion. Through the great rooms we wandered, filled with rich mahogany furniture carved by the black men at the native mission. Neatly dressed black boys stood about everywhere eager to serve us; in the separate kitchen at the edge of the luxuriant garden the cook and his two assistants waited for our commands.

"Home was never like this," I said to Alice gayly. "No ambassador could ask for more. Even one with a full portfolio."

We walked out to the back yard where the Congo boiled and churned like dirty coffee, preparing to descend the nearby rapids. A huge crocodile arose from the mud as we approached, joined an instant later by an even larger companion. Our princely home was in the middle of a crocodile promenade.

40

We showered, and dressing hastily, were driven to the elaborate dinner the High Commissioner had arranged in honor of our coming. We sat down at a long table under the stars. Above us the drooping fronds of the palm trees swayed gently; giant moths and praying mantis flew constantly before our faces, attracted by the sputtering acetylene lamps set on the immaculate cloth. There were perhaps forty officers present, the High Command of the Free French rebels in Africa, and their close associates.

I had been introduced to them one by one—the quiet General De Larminat, the gentle-voiced General Sicé. But I learned within minutes that except for these two the introductions were useless. Most of the names were false. The wives and children of the majority of these men were still in Germany or Vichy France; a hint of the activities in which their husbands or fathers were engaged would have meant prison—or worse.

It was a gay dinner, with the conversation as merry as the jolliest student party I had attended in the young, carefree days when I lived on a side street of the Left Bank near the Boulevard Saint-Michel in Paris. There was no hint that every man at the table was a hero who had risked his life to arrive.

I was talking with General De Larminat next me, and was about to try a spoonful of the thick soup a black boy set before me, when Lieutenant Laurelle, a few chairs away, took a tiny cardboard box from his pocket.

41

He caught my eye and sent the box down the table. "Your quinine, Monsieur. The Brazzaville caviar."

I took a capsule with a grimace and passed one to Alice. It was to haunt me for a long time after, that Brazzaville caviar. I can still taste its chalky bitterness even in my dreams.

As we ate, occasionally a great bat flew overhead. Whenever there was a pause in the conversation I could hear the tom-toms off in the native quarter beating dully. A long series of toasts followed the dessert, spoken in beautiful literary French. But for me most of their beauty was wasted. I am one of those unfortunate mortals whose blood seems to have an irresistible fascination for any biting insect, particularly the mosquito. Under the table the mosquitoes were eating me alive.

The dinner ended. We returned to our dignified mansion, and went into the back yard for a look at the turbulent Congo, now a mass of silvery foam under a brilliant moon. A giant crocodile reared up out of the shadows. We retreated inside the house hastily, and vowed we would make no more such nightly excursions.

We undressed and crept beneath our mosquito nets. The air in the room, even with its high ceiling, was stifling; in a moment my pajamas and the sheets were dripping with perspiration. We lay there unable to sleep, talking quietly, until late into the night, as people might talk in a Turkish bath. Outside on the doorstep I could hear one of the houseboys playing an African piano, a curious instrument hardly larger than a man's hand, with a liquid, melancholy tone like the song of a mournful bird. Off in the distance the tom-toms were beating louder now, in sharp staccato rhythm as though for a dance. A faint breeze began to blow off the water. Through the windows there drifted the smell of swamps and fetid crocodiles and rotting forests old as time, the smell of Africa.

We awoke in the morning with an excited chattering outside. Pulling away the mosquito net I saw two sleek young chimpanzees high in the branches of the papaya tree next door, stripping off the golden fruit and stuffing it into their mouths, while a white man below, obviously their master, called out fervent pleas and maledictions.

We dressed and went down to our regal dining room for breakfast. We were having our coffee when Lieutenant Laurelle arrived to take us on our first day's inspection. The lieutenant, I learned, for a considerable time had been a New York resident. His point of view, his manners were so intensely American, he might have passed at an advertising convention as a typical executive of Madison Avenue.

He picked up the telephone to call the High Commissioner's office. And then I made my first acquaintance with the difficulties of war in Africa. The line was as dead as though electricity had never been discovered.

Laurelle sighed with resignation. "The telephone is bad enough. But the telegraph is worse. Major Clapot tried an experiment a few weeks ago. He sent a message by the electric telegraph to a point eighty miles distant in the jungle, and the same message to the same place by the native tom-tom. The tom-tom beat the telegraph by two and a half hours."

He took us on a quick tour of the town, and I was made aware of my first Congo miracle. I had noticed at the dinner that the food was superb. I discovered that the sole reason was the magic of French cooking. For as we went about I learned at once the grim truth. Brazzaville and the French Congo, always remote in the best of times, now that they were cut off from the motherland like rebellious children, had nothing. There were none of the supplies so necessary to support life for a white man in this fearful climate; the shelves in the tiny shops, the army warehouses, were empty. There was no butter and no milk. The tsetse fly made keeping cows impossible. All meat came from long distances; by the time it arrived often it was so stony it could not be eaten.

But it was an exciting place, with soldiers, black and white, marching everywhere through the palm-fringed streets, training to renew the battle against the Germans. Most of the white soldiers were extraordinarily young, some almost boys, as though it were a revolt of youth against the defeatism of the old men of Vichy.

The miracle of the cooking was repeated in the soldiers' equipment. When the first men arrived there had been no weapons. They dredged up some condemned rifles and machine guns dumped long ago into the Congo and with oil and painstaking labor made them workable again. From empty gasoline drums they produced canteens and mess kits; from automobile tires thrown on the dump heap they made soldiers' shoes. The Vichy government sent three bombers to blast them into submission. They brought the planes down with their remade rifles and machine guns. Out of the three wrecks they made one plane, literally tied together with string and wire, which was now their pride and joy. It was also the entire Brazzaville Air Force.

I ended the morning at the Camp D'Ornano where student officers were drilling on a muddy field, young heroes like the others escaped from France, and sworn never to rest until the last German was driven from its soil. At the request of the commandant I made a speech, full I am sure of dull and unoriginal remarks about patriotism and nobility and courage. But they were very young, and the times were very grim, and the cynicism of Paris and New York were very far away. And it was my first chance to take my ambassadorship seriously.

We left the camp and went to lunch at the home of General Sicé, who next to General De Gaulle, was the most important figure in the Free French movement. Though I had been in Brazzaville only a few hours, I had already learned his history. One of the highest medical men in the French army, a doctor rather than a soldier by nature, when most of the strictly military

45

generals accepted the bitter humiliation of the Vichy armistice, ironically it was General Sicé, the doctor, who stationed at the time in the Congo, swore to fight to the end. It was General Sicé who dashed from army post to army post and village to village in the jungle urging Frenchmen and natives alike to resist, and organized the revolt that overthrew the authority of Vichy in the region. It was General Sicé who by the sheer force of his personality saved this vital strategic area, and in the opinion of many of those who knew, like General Smuts of Churchill's War Council, thus saved Africa for the Allies. When General De Gaulle issued his own plea for rebellion, thanks to General Sicé, the African training ground was ready.

There are few persons in the world who at first sight cause the observer to remark to himself, "There is a great man." As I sat with General Sicé that day, glancing at his rugged Breton face, I felt I was looking at the man who might fairly be called the French Lincoln.

He held up a china pot out of which he had poured a queer smelling liquid. "Have some citronelle tea, cher ami," he urged me. "It is good for the liver."

I tried it and found it so horrible I decided my liver must take second place to my stomach. I took a drink of Scotch instead. I watched the French officers drinking the same whisky and reflected on the curious tricks a war plays on humanity. Because these men had cut themselves off from their fellows they could get none of their beloved wine, only this brownish alcohol flavored with smoke sent by their English allies from South Africa. It was shocking to me, an ancient inhabitant of the Left Bank, to see Frenchmen drinking whisky, and though they did not complain, their wry faces told the unhappy story. I am sure this is responsible for Scotch being so fashionable in France today. For the Frenchman has a sensitive tongue and palate trained for generations on the most delicate liqueurs; only his reverence for a patriotic tradition would make him deliberately choose such a terrible drink as Scotch.

My reflections were interrupted by Lieutenant Laurelle thrusting toward me the inevitable cardboard box. "You have forgotten, Monsieur. Your ration of caviar."

I lunched with General Sicé and his friends each day thereafter, and each day learned more and more of the Vichy treachery. The truth was becoming quickly evident. The Pétain many Americans believed to be a hero fighting nobly for a lost cause, was a weak old man, who like those about him was royalist and totalitarian by nature; he and his associates preferred to deal with a foreign dictatorship which held similar authoritarian views rather than trust their own people in a democracy. Occasionally at the table some impressive figure would sit down beside me and be introduced as a Parisian gentleman called Dupont or Duval, names as common in France as Smith or Jones in America. Later I would learn he held some post in the Vichy government or served perhaps as a senator in the Vichy parliament. After infinite planning and incredible risks he had managed to steal away unnoticed and would soon go back to his pretended duties as a sort of Scarlet Pimpernel, to rescue French patriots in prison and bring them out to their friends.

Each day new refugees kept arriving, scholars and aristocrats, peasants and fishermen, sailors and carpenters, bakers and doctors and pale bank clerks. Each day was a new melodrama, a melodrama inside the greater melodrama of the war. Any war is a melodrama, in which we are the actors, playing in ever-changing scenes on a constantly shifting stage. Undoubtedly this is the reason war is so attractive to men of little minds who have no other excitement in their lives and forget the appalling consequences. This particular act of the war, laid against a background of weird witch-doctors and trumpeting elephants, broke all the rules of good theater. Too many thrilling things were happening at the same minute.

Often on the radio I could hear a message in secret code going out to some escaping camel troops in the burning Vichy-held deserts of Senegal, to help them find their perilous way across the Sahara to Free French Fort Lamy in the Tchad or British territory in Nigeria; then later I could hear the Vichy radio sending out orders to stop them at any cost. Sometimes they arrived safely, and those about me would rejoice; sometimes there was only silence and we knew they had either been captured or

died of thirst. On several occasions a merry combat officer I encountered at mess turned out to be a Catholic
priest who had changed his Bible and beads for a rifle.
Once a quiet, deep-tanned soldier proved to be a convict
escaped from a cell on Devil's Island, ready to give his
life, if necessary, for the country which had condemned
him to perpetual captivity.

There could no longer be any doubt as to the truth. I
hurried over to the tiny telegraph office to send my first
dispatch. Carefully the black soldier at the key, with no
knowledge of what he was sending, tapped out each letter telling America how France, believed dead beyond
hope of resurrection, was being reborn thousands of
miles away in the jungles of Africa. The heart of France,
tapped the black finger, was no longer in Paris along the
gentle Seine; it was here in Brazzaville, along the banks
of the fever-ridden Congo.

I saw the result when I looked at my first American
newspapers ten months later. A double banner front
page headline in the *New York World-Telegram* and
shortly after a similar story in the *Reader's Digest*. It
was the newspaperman's dream of a lifetime, a world
scoop.

With my duties as a journalist temporarily disposed
of, I had time to think of my other responsibility—that
of Ambassador. I prepared a long telegram to Tony
Biddle in London, pointing out the strategic position of
the Free French in preventing a German sweep down

from North Africa. It was a military axiom that the Tchad was the keystone of Africa. If the Free French lost it to the enemy, there was nothing to prevent the Nazi tanks from seizing the mineral riches of the Belgian Congo and splitting the continent in two. Even more important was the psychological value of creating a resistance inside France itself. I concluded by stating in restrained language fitting for a diplomat, that if we did not come to the rescue of these courageous rebels, we were little short of crazy.

There was an American consul across the Stanley Pool in Leopoldville, an amiable individual whose chief duties consisted of stamping missionary passports, and despite the wilting heat that made a new bath necessary before the water of the old one had dried, attending Belgian functions in top hat and tails. We had met several times in a casual way; it was instantly obvious that he had been instructed to avoid the Free French as he would avoid a colony of malignant lepers.

I took the ferry with the telegram in my pocket, and making my way to the building with the American eagle over the doorway, asked the consul if he could send my message; because of its contents it was vital that it be sent in code.

He looked at its two close-typed pages and gave a gasp of horror. "Good God!" he exclaimed. "It's impossible. It would use up my telegraph allowance for twenty years!"

I thought of his instructions to beware of the lepers, and the mountains of dull consular briefs and missionary passports among which he must spend his life, and I knew the case was hopeless.

But a good ambassador does not accept defeat so easily.

In Brazzaville I had conversed several times with British Consul General Parr, an astute if somewhat odd English civil servant direct from the pages of Somerset Maugham, who was in effect the British Minister to the Free French in Africa.

I hurried back across the river and taking a pouspous, called on Mr. Parr at his office. As he sat reading my telegram I thought how he was precisely the type of Briton who on a lonely island would have his copies of the *London Times*, which arrived all together once a year, set before him at breakfast each morning in the proper numerical succession; though he might never see a white man, he would invariably dress each night for dinner.

He looked up from the typed pages with his usual cryptic smile. "Perfect," he said. "I'll send it at once."

So it happened that the first on-the-spot report about the Free French to the American State Department was made through a Somerset Maugham British Consul by a wandering Kentucky-born Mississippi River novelist traveling with money paid him by Paramount Pictures.

My first diplomatic mission was thus accomplished.

I waited impatiently to see what would happen as a result.

Our days in Brazzaville passed swiftly. Each noon we ate with General Sicé in his unpretentious home, for he hated ostentation; each day, as we were served by his faithful black servant Boko, I fought off drinking the evil-smelling citronelle tea. Now and then I went off for lunch with the quiet General De Larminat or the far more loquacious Félix Eboué, the brilliant, idealistic Negro who as Governor of the Tchad was one of the first to respond to General Sicé's pleas, and was now the Governor of the Congo.

At night we sometimes dined with the pink-cheeked young Englishmen of the Speers Mission, established as a liaison between the French rebels and the British after General Speers at Churchill's request had brought De Gaulle in his plane from Paris to London. They were an attractive lot, Brian Guinness and the others, young aristocrats fresh from English universities. It was pleasant to spend a few hours speaking my own language after struggling all day in complex French.

Moreover we were sure of a good dinner, unlikely if we ate at home. For the black cook who presided over the kitchen of our royal establishment was generally drunk on the native palm wine and our meals reflected his libations.

Sometimes we and our French and British friends would all dine together. There was no slightest hint of the volcanic explosion in which I was to be caught a few months later in the far-off, mysterious Druse Mountains of Syria, an explosion with incalculable consequences to France and England and the entire war.

At these meals and elsewhere I began to hear more and more queer stories of the weird things that happened in the primitive world beyond the town, of evil witch doctors, and leopard men, and cannibals who ate their own sisters and mothers. Not long before our arrival two old women near Brazzaville had been executed for the ritual murder of a girl of seven; they had believed that by the evil magic of her death they could acquire their long-lost youth again.

Only a short walk from our gateway brought the wanderer to dense jungles waiting to close in about the settlement like a horde of hungry jackals. Let the white man and the black move away, and soon all traces of their existence would have vanished. There would be only the trees drooping with scaly lianas and the ants and the crocodiles.

Often as I lay in bed at night and heard the tom-tom beating mysteriously, I thought how strange it was that France, so long a leader in culture and intellect should have its rebirth in this savage wilderness, better fitted for leopards and elephants.

I began to hear more and more as well of a certain Colonel Leclerc, a twentieth-century D'Artagnan off in the Sahara, from which he made spectacular forays on

53

the terrified Italian garrisons south of the Libyan desert. From all reports the region between Brazzaville and the area where he made his attacks was the wildest part of the Dark Continent, still almost as primitive and unknown as it had existed in the days of the early explorers. This was the Africa no other American had ever penetrated. This would really be the Africa of my book with the padded cover.

I determined, when my stay in Brazzaville was over, to seek out this mythical Leclerc and see if the legends were true.

I continued to send my dispatches about the Vichy treachery and the events along the Congo, so remote, yet so vital to the war. I was bursting with enthusiasm now and cabled everyone of importance I knew in America, urging them to help the Free French patriots before it was too late. Soon I received the welcome news that my stories, reprinted widely in magazines and newspapers, were deeply undermining Vichy support. At the same time news spread in the usual mysterious ways of the contents of my cable to Tony Biddle.

The reaction in Brazzaville to the dispatches and my diplomatic report was startling. Before I was merely a well-disposed journalist. Now I was a fighting champion. No door was closed if I wished to enter, no information was too secret to be withheld. My writings, translated, were broadcast on the Brazzaville radio directed into Vichy territory to the North and West, and beamed on the BBC into Paris. I shared in the conferences planning to create a resistance in France itself. A new Vichy official arrived at the risk of his life to bring his priceless knowledge of the Pétain hierarchy. I glowed with pride when General Sicé, calling the visitor by his real name, introduced me as "our trusted writer."

Now I was a full-fledged conspirator, beyond my wildest dreams.

I returned one afternoon to our house to find the usually jovial Major Clapot waiting for me, nervously pacing up and down the flowered veranda.

"*Ah, mon cher*, there is grave trouble," he said. "When we gave you General De Gaulle's house to live in we thought that at this time there was no possibility of the General's coming to Brazzaville. We have just received a radiogram. The General is arriving by plane early to-morrow morning."

I replied there was a strong possibility the General might like to have his house, inasmuch as for the time being it would also become the headquarters of the entire Free French movement.

Laurelle came a few moments later. There was a hasty conference, followed by numerous calls over the erratic telephone. It was arranged at last that the Attorney General take us as his guests for the few days of De Gaulle's visit. Feverishly we went about the many rooms of the rambling building, collecting our varied belongings. It was no easy task, for the Major had told us to make ourselves at home and I had taken his words literally. On two or three occasions some French dignitary had stayed in a distant part of the house, for perhaps forty-eight hours. But these individuals had come in like ghosts, late at night and left again almost at dawn, leaving no more mark of their presence than if they had been one of the wandering spirits of the drowned men our black boys constantly saw prowling the banks of the river. But no real occupant had ever disputed our sovereignty.

My manuscripts, my pens and typewriter ribbons, Alice's paints and tracing paper and drawings were scattered everywhere. There was no dresser drawer in a bedroom that failed to contain a shirt or a pair of socks or some intimate bit of lady's lingerie, no table that was not piled high with pastel-smeared sketch pads or smudgy carbon copies of my dispatches. It was a dwelling now much more suitable for two untidy Bohemians in Greenwich Village or Montmartre than the austere needs of a French general.

We moved to the pleasant residence of the Attorney General about midnight. I slept a few hours and wakened early to go out with General Sicé and my other friends to greet General De Gaulle at the shabby little airport. De Gaulle, wearing a cork hat like the other generals, invited me to come and have tea with him that afternoon at five o'clock. The meeting place would be, of course, his house on the Congo.

I arrived promptly as is my habit, and was met at the

door by one of the General's aides who courteously ushered me into the house—*my* house. An instant later the lanky De Gaulle himself appeared, and with ceremonial politeness received me in the living room—*my* living room. Then he led me into the study—*my* study, sat down at *my* desk, and offered me a cigarette—one of *my* cigarettes I had left the night before.

I learned then how deep-seated is that instinct so common to all of us—squatters' rights. I resented the General's reception, however polite. I felt I should be receiving General De Gaulle.

4.
General De Gaulle
Serves Tea

My talk with the General started in this amusing fashion. It ended by becoming the most uncomfortable hour and a half of my life.

The visit, I had been informed, was to be part interview, part a formal thanks to me for making the Free French and De Gaulle known to America. As he gave me a cup of tea, I studied him closely. He was a striking figure as he sat there, of extraordinary height, even in his chair; he seemed at first far more like a reserved Englishman than the usual conception of the electric Frenchman.

We talked about inconsequential matters for a moment, and then he made a revelation that came with the suddenness of a bomb dropped out of the hot African sky. I had asked what caused him to rebel against the Vichy surrender.

"There was no other way," he answered. "It was not a matter of minutes, not a matter of a quick decision. The debacle was a long time in coming. I saw it arriving. More than that, I saw the debacle being prepared."

He sat silent an instant in thought. "As you remember, when Marshal Pétain took over the supreme command of the Army all France believed he was going to rally the great powers of the country to resist the Germans. That was his first duty, the purpose for which he was appointed to the post. Unfortunately his actions were exactly the contrary. At that time I was in the War

59

Office. I shall never forget the occasion when Pétain arrived from his first conference with Premier Reynaud. To my astonishment, instead of advancing plans for halting the enemy, with his first words he urged that Reynaud ask for an armistice. 'We are finished,' he said. 'We must capitulate.' Remember, this was almost a full month before the armistice, when the resisting powers of France were still enormous. From that moment, every time he saw Reynaud, at every slightest opportunity, he continued to repeat his plea. 'France is done. We must surrender.' Even if matters had been going well instead of badly the psychological effect would have been disastrous. For a general supposed to be defending his country, an officer of the French Army whose tradition was to die before surrender, his attitude was beyond belief."

He turned to speak to his adjutant who came in with a message, and went on. "I tried to argue with Pétain, and one of my colleagues in the War Office joined me. 'France must resist,' we pleaded. 'Even if the Germans sweep across all France we can fight delaying actions as long as possible, and then carry on the fight from the colonies.'

"But each time Pétain would deny us. 'You are young,' he would tell us again and again. 'What you are saying is silly, puerile. I am an old experienced military man and I know. The war is over.'"

I asked if De Gaulle had any explanation of Pétain's extraordinary conduct.

"It lies in the personality of Pétain," he answered. "I

60

have known him a long time. Pétain is of the old French military school, brought up in the tradition of the Franco-Prussian War of 1870. When the mechanized war of 1939 arrived he could not see any difference. He tried to fight it with the strategy of seventy years before. Moreover he was always a pessimist; he always saw only the dark side of an affair."

A black boy came into the room to bring us more tea.

De Gaulle stirred his cup in reflection. "And so when Pétain took over the government, and had the power in his hands, he asked for the armistice."

I should have been very happy at the interview. De Gaulle's revelations were both sensational and in perfect accord with what I had been thinking and writing. I knew they would make a sensational newspaper story in America. His disclosures were borne out by what I had learned elsewhere. I had heard from some of the officers in Brazzaville how they suspected that they had been removed from posts of high command in France so the treasonable pact with the Germans could be more easily accomplished. I had heard of Pétain's profound royalist sympathies and his great personal ambition.

But instead of being happy I was troubled as I had never been troubled before. For the General himself came as a terrific shock. I had heard he was an egotist. I was totally unprepared for the truth. There was an intellectual arrogance in his speech and manner, a disdain for the rest of humanity such as I had never encountered in a human being. Here was a man so wrapped up in his own consciousness it was as if no one else in the world existed. I agreed completely with every word he spoke. But they were uttered with a bitterness, a fanaticism that might lead anywhere.

He stopped talking about Pétain, and I could see that he was trying to thank me for my efforts with my own countrymen. But he gave me the feeling that for him any expression of gratitude was impossible. We give thanks to God, but God takes us for granted.

I left him and walked down the drowsy street. The responsibility of a sincere journalist at times can be appalling. Through an extraordinary combination of circumstances I was the only writer within thousands of miles, and because of that fact had been able to make the Free French and De Gaulle sympathetically known to my countrymen. There was no other correspondent to say, in effect, that I was a liar, no one to keep my opinion from being accepted as gospel. I had created in America the legend of De Gaulle, the patriot fighting the dictators. Now after meeting the reality, I had a feeling I might have made a terrible mistake. I wondered if I had created, unknowing, a new Frankenstein monster, a possible Fascist, who when he achieved power would be little better than the dictators he sought to overthrow?

Yet if I expressed my fears, it was only too clear what would happen. The Vichy lobby in Washington I knew, was enormously powerful, and the pro-Vichy policy of the American government was as strong as ever. If I, the champion of the Free French, publicly attacked the leader, all the good I had accomplished would be wasted. The struggling rebel cause, which I felt so vital to the winning of the war, would be harmed irreparably. Dangerous factions would be created, and many Americans, hitherto friendly, would turn away, disappointed. Surrounded by so many powerful enemies, as far as its existence in America was concerned, the movement might very well collapse.

That night I lay awake for hours under my stifling net, while the mosquitoes buzzed incessantly, trying to make up my mind about a course of action. I reminded myself that in time of battle the defenders inside a beleaguered fort do not turn their guns inward but outward. And there was one fact that gave me a shred of hope. This was De Gaulle's liberal attitude toward the black peoples of French Africa and his plan to incorporate them some day into a French union as sovereign states, rather than as colonies, an attitude in startling contrast to his dictatorial personality. I decided that I would keep my innermost thoughts to myself, and writing the interview as fairly as I could, put down the facts, without any dubious personal interpretation. Meanwhile I would hope that my impressions were wrong or that De Gaulle would change in the future.

I was glad next morning I had made this decision,

when I went with the others to the drab parade ground and saw him inspect the pitiful little group of soldiers that formed this important part of the Free French Army. Heroes, I have found in my experience, rarely look like heroes. The uniforms of the men were faded and their shoes ill-fitting; their rifles would have seemed more appropriate for a group of guerrillas, fighting in some far-off part of China, rather than for the soldiers of what had been one of the greatest armies in the world. As De Gaulle, tall and stiff as a native spear marched in front of the ranks frozen to attention, he was followed by a dilapidated, flea-bitten dog who had wandered unnoticed onto the field, one of those forlorn descendants of the wild jackals who had somehow survived the bite of the tsetse. It was almost as though the dog were a devoted worshiper, trying to imitate his idol. When the General took a step forward the dog stepped forward also. When the General halted the dog came to a stop as well, taking advantage of the pause to scratch a particularly troublesome flea. Each salute to the General he took as though it were his own. He followed to the base of a wooden tier of seats and watched patiently while the General climbed onto a platform and began a speech in his rich, magnetic voice, calling again as he had called before, on Frenchmen everywhere to resist. The dog listened politely until the oration was finished, then stole off into the mysterious reaches from which he had come. He was one of those symbols which delight the philosopher: beside the king or the emperor, there so often marches an absurd caricature.

The General left the following morning, and we returned to our white-verandaed home we had so hastily abandoned.

I have thought many times of those days of the General's visit. If the American government had not opposed the Free French movement so foolishly, so blindly, I would certainly have written what I felt; many important Free Frenchmen who I found later had the same deep misgivings would have expressed their opinions in the same way. De Gaulle would probably have been replaced by General Sicé, and never come to the command of France, and modern history would have been different.

But more of the lean General later in the explosion.

I continued my investigations. As I talked to the refugees and the soldiers drilling under the blistering sun, the reasons for the tragic fall of France became clearer and clearer. There were many contributing causes: the terrible French losses in the First World War that made the French people reluctant to think about the possibility of a second holocaust: the Maginot Line psychology that let Frenchmen sleep peacefully, thinking they were safe behind an impregnable wall of steel; the failure of the French High Command to mechanize their troops when the Germans were bringing their army to mechanized perfection.

But most important of all in their country's ruin were the corrupt politicians and the Fascist-minded industrialists and officers who were still spiritually eating at the regal tables of Marie Antoinette, and holding their conferences in the gilded palace halls of the Bourbons. Again and again in the stories of their evil plotting there cropped up the once revered name of Marshal Pétain. Not long afterward I met a non-French diplomat of international fame and importance. With the strict promise that I would never reveal his identity, he told me that only three months after the outbreak of the war in 1939, there came to him the appalling news of a plot being hatched by royalist and Fascist groups in France to overthrow the government and make a separate peace with Germany. He investigated and found the report to be true in every detail; the instigators were certain traitorous French industrialists who were admirers of Adolf Hitler. The man they planned to ask to head the new state was Marshal Pétain.

Months later I came on irrefutable proof, a little paper-bound book called "It's Pétain That We Need," ("C'Est Pétain Que Nous Faut") published by a Fascist society in France, with full details of how a Fascist coup could be managed and ending with these prophetic sentences: "In time of peace such a coup is difficult. In time of war it is easy." It detailed the constitution such a government was to adopt. The date of the book's publication was 1933, six years before the outbreak of the war. The constitution it proposed was almost phrase by phrase the constitution of the new Vichy state under Marshal Pétain.

There was a momentary respite in my political activities when I received an invitation to make a quick trip to some of the territories that lay beyond Brazzaville; it would give me a chance to penetrate the mysterious forest of which I had heard so many tales. We set out in an army pickup truck soon after. I sat beside the driver and watched fascinated as we plunged deeper and deeper into the somber colonnades of trees. The forest became a matted jungle; eagerly I waited to see some sign, to hear some voice close at hand such as might have come to Alan Quatermain or the other mythical African explorers in whose adventures as a boy I had lost myself, something that would help reveal to me the soul of Africa.

I had not long to wait. We had arrived after several hours at a plantation chopped out of the wilderness, and were strolling about with the elderly French proprietress when a thick reddish stream of what appeared to be oil or molasses spilling from a broken drum showed in the path ahead. Alice, who happened to be nearest, was about to take a step toward it when the French woman, just behind, seized her arm and pulled her back in fright.

"Look out!" she cried. "The manion ants!"

I hurried up to examine these fierce insects, the dread man-eaters of the jungle. They were small ants, perhaps half an inch long, like shiny slivers of reddish mica. Relentlessly they moved over the ground in close-packed ranks like an iron-disciplined army, with tough sergeants on either side to butt any stragglers brutally back into line. I had heard how sometimes they had passed a plantation house for three days and three nights and still showed no sign of ending; when they reached a village, if their path was not barred by trenches filled with fire, not a rat or a chicken or a cockroach or even a slow-moving human being would be left alive.

The French woman shuddered, as she led the way back to the plantation house. She spoke sadly, "They are devils, these ants. I had a pet chimpanzee here that I loved like a child. I kept him at night in his own little house just outside my bedroom window, on a chain so that he would not destroy the papayas. A few nights ago I wakened and heard the chain rattle. I thought the chimpanzee was playing as he often played, so I did not get up to see if anything was the matter. In the morning I went out to free him and give him his breakfast as usual and I saw the manion had come in the night. There was only the chimpanzee's chain and a pile of white bones."

I had learned my second lesson. Africa was cruel.

We arrived another day as night fell at a jungle cross-roads, having missed our connection because of a telegraph line pulled down by an elephant. The only shelter was a weather-beaten, long-abandoned shed set on a slight elevation at the edge of the forest. Lightning

68

began to flash ominously; the black boys, worried about the weather, hurried inside with our army cots and set them up near the door.

By the flickering light of the kerosene lantern we could see an odd, flowered pattern on the battered ceiling and walls.

Alice studied the design curiously. "Queer anyone having daisy patterned wallpaper here," she commented.

As she spoke the daisies suddenly began to move. They were hairy spiders numbered in the thousands.

I had learned my third lesson. In Africa there was rarely one of any creature, animal or insect. If animals they usually came by the scores, if insects they came by the hundreds and millions.

We went on another day to Pointe Noire, once known as Luango, where in the cruel days of the slave trade, so many black men and women were shipped in chains to the cottonfields of America. Now it was the busy port of Free French Africa where war supplies from Britain and South Africa that escaped the marauding submarines, were shipped off to the interior. The Governor took us to call on the king of Luango, a chunky, good-natured black man, for a long time, legend said, a pastry cook in a French home, but now restored on a straw throne in all his royal splendor.

That night we drove with the Governor to the nearby forest to see a show the king had arranged of the magic of his chief witch doctors. Quickly we took places on logs made into an improvised bench, while perhaps a hundred black men, each holding a flickering torch, gathered about us in a wide circle. Before them a score of Negroes, holding drums and metal rods, squatted on the spongy ground, with a close-packed mass of other black men and women squatting near them, mere spectators, chattering excitedly.

At a signal the drums began to beat; the metal rods clanged rhythmically. The murmuring crowd grew silent, tense with expectation. Suddenly from the blackness of the forest two Negroes darted forward with a blood-curdling cry and halted theatrically before us. For a moment they stood motionless as statues, two towering giants over six feet tall, each wearing only a breech clout and red feathers in his hair, their black polished bodies luridly reflecting the flames of the distant torches. The beat of the drums grew wilder, the clang of the metal rods became deafening. One of the giants, whose body was marked with a curious tattooing, held up a bit of vine near his mouth, and pretending to swallow it with fantastic grimaces, began to act as though he were working it down his body. Across his chest it moved, past his stomach and waist and thighs, always to the accompaniment of cries of unbearable agony. It reached his knee and halted for a time, striking some immovable obstacle, then went on again at last, and reached the black ankle. With a new flourish the witch doctor daubed some white paint on the foot beneath, and seizing a stone knife, slashed quickly at the whitened flesh. The blood spurted out like a crimson spring. With a final cry of triumph, the sorcerer stooped and pulled the vine from the wound, his gestures, the pleased expression on his face, exactly those of a vaudeville trouper playing the opening magic act to a crowded house at the old Palace Theater on Broadway. But there was one grim difference in the audience. Here the actor had the power of life and death.

The black people about us fell on their faces in awe.

We returned to Brazzaville.

"This is nothing," said General Sicé with a smile when I had made my report. "Wait until you go up the river to visit Leclerc. Then you will see the real Africa."

"I hope you and your wife are tough," added Laurelle. "It's a trip even few Frenchmen have taken. It is not exactly a journey to Connecticut."

Our stay in Brazzaville was suddenly shortened by far-away events. The war news, dismal enough when we left America, had grown appalling. Germany had overrun Hungary and invaded Yugoslavia and Greece. London and Coventry had been subjected to frightful air raids and the vital port cities were under an almost continuous rain of bombs. The losses from the U-boats had become staggering. Operating in wolf packs, attacking from all directions, in three months they had sunk over 800,000 tons of shipping. It seemed almost impossible that England could survive.

Even worse, from our personal point of view, was

the situation developing in the sandy wastes along the coasts of Libya and Egypt where I planned to journey after staying with Leclerc at the far-off settlement of Fort Lamy, which I had learned was his headquarters in the Tchad. The British, jubilant after an initial triumph in North Africa, had been driven back by the newly-arrived Rommel and forced to evacuate Benghazi with frightful losses. The German general's armored columns were moving farther and farther across the desert toward Cairo. If we did not start soon his rumbling tanks might at any moment sweep on to the Nile and make our expedition impossible.

"I've been thinking it over," remarked Laurelle as we sat with General Sicé for our usual lunch discussing our plans for the journey. "You aren't twenty-one. And it will be very hard on your wife. The trip across country is too rough and too dangerous. You had better go by plane."

But General Sicé shook his graying head. "Let them go the way they like. They will realize the difficulties our soldiers face. And they will see the true Africa they could learn in no other way. They will know the Heart of Darkness."

We began our preparations for departure. We renewed our supply of quinine and any other drugs the almost empty commissary could supply, for the area through which we were to pass was one of the worst disease-ridden in the world, full of blackwater fever and sleeping sickness and elephantiasis and leprosy, and a score of somber diseases whose very names are a blank to those who live in happier climates. On our last night we gave a farewell dinner for all our friends, General Sicé, Laurelle, Clapot, Brian Guinness and his pink-cheeked associates, and Consul General Parr. As always it was a gay affair. At the height of the festivities Masamba, our tiny, white-turbaned black boy, came up to my chair at the head of the table solemnly carrying a dead snake on a stick.

"O Master, I have just killed it in the garden," he announced, full of pride. "It is the terrible minute snake. If it had bitten you, Master, in sixty seconds you would have died."

In the morning I sent my last dispatches; off in the wilderness where we were heading it would be weeks before I could send a telegram again. A few days before, I had been given a roundabout message from Tony Biddle saying that he had received my favorable report and had forwarded it to Washington. But there had been no slightest sign of any change in policy; no faintest indication of any aid to these brave men struggling to put France back into the war. In spite of my qualms about De Gaulle, my enthusiasm for the Free French cause grew ever stronger. I decided that in the future I would concentrate some of my press fire on Washington and see if I could bring about some practical result.

We were piling the last of our belongings into our suitcases when a long melancholy whistle sounded down the water. An instant later Laurelle drove up in his car, accompanied by the ruddy Clapot. We climbed inside, and hurrying off to tell General Sicé goodbye, sped down to the tiny Brazzaville dock. A white painted steamboat was anchored there with twin columns of smoke pouring out the lofty stacks, like the steamboats I knew so well on my own Mississippi. But instead of the usual cotton bales piled on the decks, there were now cases of ammunition; instead of passengers on a river holiday there were red-uniformed soldiers bound for war.

I had learned at dinner the night before that in some of the areas where we would be traveling Alice would be the first white woman to enter. I would be the first white man not a French soldier or government official. André Gide had journeyed part of the way in peace time. But even he had not reached some of the regions I would be exploring. This time I could really feel like Stanley, the Boula Matadi, the great Breaker of Stones.

We hurried aboard with a troop of grinning black boys trudging behind us, carrying our baggage on their heads. Laurelle disappeared for a moment into a cabin, returning with a lavish bunch of roses in his arms. With one of the charming speeches for which he was famous, he presented Alice with the bouquet. As the whistle blew again in final warning, he and Major Clapot shook our hands and hurried onto the dock.

There followed a great commotion down in the hull

and a fierce clanking of machinery and hissing of steam. But the great paddlewheel did not turn; the boat remained motionless. The Captain spoke to me unhappily. Something had gone wrong with the engine.

For an hour we lay there with the sun beating down upon us mercilessly, while Laurelle and Clapot with the genial pessimism of soldiers, called out bantering remarks to help us on our way.

"You'll never get to Fort Lamy, *mon cher*," called Laurelle. "I told you to take the plane."

"Even if the boat ever goes you've started your trip a month too late," called Clapot. "The rainy season's on, and the trails will be one big lake. You'll be back here in two weeks."

"You know the old proverb," shouted Laurelle. "In Africa sometimes you know when you're starting. But you never know when you're arriving . . . We'll have the plane waiting."

Suddenly there came a curious muffled sound I had known since my childhood, unlike any other sound in the world, the rhythmic sighing of the stacks of a Mississippi steamboat. The paddlewheel began to churn in a white Niagara of foam; the lumbering vessel began to move slowly from the dock.

The two officers waved their helmets.

"Don't forget your caviar!" called Laurelle.

The waving helmets disappeared around a bend.

The boat steamed slowly up the Congo.

II.
THE
EXPLORER

5.
Prisoners of the Jungle

The Captain, a tall, powerfully-built Frenchman with a serious manner unusual in those of his calling, took us on a tour of inspection. The boat, named the Fondère, was a comfortable craft, almost identical in size and architecture with the old-time packets on the Mississippi. On the main deck were cabins for the first-class passengers and the Captain and his gay Parisian wife who, clad in smart blouse and shorts, supervised the kitchen; on the deck below were perhaps 150 soldiers, like ourselves on their way eventually to join Leclerc.

Quickly we met the occupants of the cabins adjoining ours: army officers, like the soldiers, journeying to the Sahara; a silvery-haired infantry captain smoking a volcanic pipe and a bearded sergeant of the Foreign Legion who boomed out his words like thunder; a stout, jovial Viennese surgeon, revolted by Hitler's seizure of his country, who smelt faintly of iodoform; a French artillery major with a husky voice little more than a whisper, still undergoing treatment to arrest the sleeping sickness he had contracted in the pestilential jungle where we were heading.

Foamily the great paddlewheel labored, pushing the boat up the water. The wide Stanley Pool ended. Beside us now on either shore were enormous walls of trees, two hundred feet high, and matted with lianas sometimes thick as a man's hand. We were passing through the great equatorial rain forest, which broken by a few clearings,

79

stretched from the Atlantic to the mountains of East Africa. Crocodiles appeared everywhere along the bank, and long-legged birds so thin and wiry they seemed two-dimensional birds cut from white paper. Now and then the blunt nostrils of a hippopotamus ploughed through the murky current. From the forest there came again the musty smell of Africa.

The boat slackened its speed. An old riverman, I guessed we were approaching a shoal.

Two glistening Negroes moved to the wide bow of the boat, and dipping long poles, began to take soundings.

"M'Tao," called the leadsman on the right, an old man wrinkled like a dried coconut. "Five."

"M'Tao," echoed the leadsman on the left, a young Negro tall and graceful as a young tree, in a voice liquid as the water below him.

"M'Sato. Three," called the coconut.

"M'Sato," echoed the young Negro.

The old Negro watched the water intently and dipped the pole again. He swung round to the pilot. "Moko!" he called sharply. "One!"

The boat came almost to a stop. I could feel a dull grating under our hull, as if we were aground. Then the grating ceased. The boat moved cautiously forward.

"M'Bale. Two," called the old man, then in rapid succession, "M'Tao, Five. Motoba, Six." He ended with "Sambo," meaning seven, the name once so common in every old-time minstrel show.

The shoal was cleared. The boat steamed on swiftly. The leadsmen put down their poles and moved away.

A tsetse fly darted out from the trees and lighted on my arm. Before I could slap it away, it had pricked me like a needle.

"The grand lottery, Monsieur," boomed the bearded sergeant of the Legionnaires. "One in 2500 are infected, and will give you sleeping sickness. You have ticket number one."

"I hope you do not win," said the artillery major in his husky whisper. "It is not a good prize."

At the edge of the forest some native huts shaped like beehives appeared, much like those we had seen at the mouth of the Congo. Beyond we could hear the muffled sound of drums.

Along the bank were tall mounds of firewood, cut in even lengths to feed our boat's hungry boilers. The vessel drifted to a stop. With a great shouting of excited voices and a soft pattering of bare feet, the black men began to bring the wood aboard, just as I had seen them so often on the lower Mississippi. It was uncanny, the way the life I knew there was repeated here in every detail. Only the background was different. There the river was sunny, cheerful; here it was dark, sinister.

We walked about the village. Here and there women were pounding *manioc* for the evening meal, and naked black children were playing with bows and arrows. In back of the huts was another group of earthen cones that

81

I thought at first were other native dwellings. As we approached, I saw they were not huts but ant-hills, twenty five to thirty feet high. Nearby in a tree, hung the nests of other ants. Beneath these, rumor said, offenders against tribal customs were tied to the trunk so the ants could be their executioners.

The boat steamed on once more. All day we traveled, while the sun beat down on the steel decks and walls with such intensity, often there came a curious scorched smell, as though the paint were burning. I felt like a baking potato in an oven, just about to burst.

Toward sunset we halted beside another village for the night. We ate and went ashore again. In the gathering dusk a trio of black men were playing long drums made of logs. A witch doctor, his body covered with ashes, his face painted to resemble a single human eye, was executing a grotesque dance, his movements at times imitating those of a rooster, at times those of a crocodile.

The quiet-mannered captain of the boat crushed a scorpion under his shoe and watched thoughtfully. "I don't know what he's up to. They're queer fellows, these witch doctors. A few of them are really wise men, who deserve their reputations. Most are racketeers and politicians, who'll do anything for a goat or a couple of chickens."

The stout Viennese surgeon nibbled a bit of chocolate. "The doctors in Brazzaville told me that some are really first-class medical men, good bone setters, with a command of drugs we don't know anything about. And they even have specialists that one village lends to another, maybe a witch doctor who specializes in clawing by a leopard or one who has his diploma for the bite of a crocodile."

An air of deep gloom lay over the settlement. I was quickly to learn they were not a happy people, most of these black men and women who dwelt along the river. For if it was the white man's tomb, it was the black man's as well. The life span in America I had heard was now nearing sixty. Here, in the great forest the average life expectancy was twenty-three. For the gods of the giant trees towering up to the skies were grim, cruel gods who brought their worshipers plagues of leprosy, and sleeping sickness, and the terrible fever that turned men yellow. And what evil the gods did not do, man himself accomplished. Before each hut grew a poison plant, set there to provide poison for arrow tips or to kill an enemy.

The witch doctor had ceased his dancing now, and the other men and women began dancing in his stead. Taking no part were a group of half a dozen Negroes with hard eyes and cruel faces.

"They may be leopard men," said the quiet Captain. "It's one of the largest secret societies, and one of the worst. They murder an enemy and then with metal claws on their hands, make it appear he was killed by a leopard.

Twenty or so were executed not far from here just a year ago."

We returned to the boat and sat listening to the war news on the radio. The situation continued to grow worse by the moment. A German-inspired revolt had broken out in Iraq, imperilling Suez and the whole Allied position in the Middle East. The German tanks during the day had made a fresh advance across North Africa and more German troops were on the way. Whether there would be a North African front for us to reach became increasingly doubtful. I thought of a dispatch I wanted to cable to the States, and asked the Captain when such a cable would be possible. He informed me I would have to wait till we arrived at Impfondu, where there was a radio in the jungle, ten days' journey away.

We went off to our cabin to sleep. I was suddenly awakened next morning by a terrible explosion and sleepily thought we might be torpedoed. I looked out the cabin door and saw it was a soldier standing by the rail almost at my head, shooting at a crocodile.

We ate breakfast. Mile after mile we traveled in a hazy dream, while the great paddlewheel churned rhythmically. Now and then a graceful native canoe glided past with black men plying long paddles, like figures magically emerged for a moment from some painting of the jungle, only to drift back into the canvas from which they had come. Occasionally a shower of sparks arose from the smokestacks, settling over the river in a fiery curtain. It reminded me of a time on the Mississippi when I was on a woodburning boat and we passed the great oil docks at Baton Rouge, and the watchmen rushed out screaming, afraid that we would set the tanks on fire. Here there were no watchmen to protest, only the birds and the hippopotamus and the ugly crocodiles. In eight hundred and fifty miles between Brazzaville and Bangui there were only twenty five Europeans, living tenuously along the river bank. Beyond the river there was nothing, only the towering, despondent trees.

We reached tsetse country now, where enormous stretches of the forest were forbidden to any human being, black or white. Here 80 per cent of the native population had been infected by the dreaded disease. I saw the victims in the villages, those in the last stages pitiful living skeletons. It took two years for the malady to run its course, ending in the final sleep from which there was no awakening. No cure was known, only a painful treatment discovered by General Sicé and two other tropical specialists that would usually arrest the disease but only if the patient kept it up the rest of his life. It was the curse of Africa. If it were ever conquered, the vast areas beside us could support huge populations. The land was among the most fertile in the world. I tried to keep Alice and myself from being bitten as much as I could. But the flies found me frequently; my collection of tickets from the lottery was growing fast.

I was never worried about the natives or the wild

animals. But I was frankly terrified of the tsetse.

My precautions redoubled. But the tsetses were cleverer than I.

A troop of large monkeys who had been swinging in the trees like star trapeze performers in a circus stopped to watch us pass. They began screaming at us wildly.

"The native's attitude toward monkeys is queer," said the silvery-haired infantry officer, enveloping us in a smoke screen from his pipe. "Some of them eat the monkey and consider him a great delicacy. Others look on him as a close relative. They would sooner eat their own brother."

The surgeon chewed a cookie. "The difference between monkeys and men is pathetically small. A colleague of mine from Brazzaville who worked in this area told me that once he sent out a call asking all the native women nursing their babies to come to his forest headquarters for some instructions. The mothers came from all directions, anxious to see the big doctor, the *Monganga Mokenge*. My friend, who is a very reliable man, swears that ten of the women had baby monkeys at their breasts."

A thundercloud appeared suddenly overhead, and a fierce tropical storm descended on the river. The Captain sent the boat into the trees, and made it fast. The storm soon ended.

Evening came. A new village showed ahead. Two

Negroes swam ashore with a rope in their free hands and carried it to a mahogany tree. We tied up for the night.

We ate supper gaily, refusing to be affected by the somber landscape. I watched in wonder the Viennese doctor eating a huge beefsteak. I had lived in Vienna, famous for its eaters. But the appetite of this Viennese was incredible. For breakfast he would have a steak, with three fried eggs on top. At ten o'clock he would have a cassecroute of steak and potatoes. At noon he would eat an enormous lunch with the others of soup and fish and meat and all the usual fattening accompaniments. At five he had an elaborate tea, at seven he enjoyed a huge dinner, and at ten o'clock before retiring prepared a lavish supper of anything he could find in the galley. I began to worry about the food supply.

The boat was moored again directly under the trees so that a great bough overhung the deck.

The sergeant of the Legion shook his bearded head. "God knows why they tie these boats so close, Monsieur," he boomed. "A perfect Champs-Elysées for the leopards. Once on a boat like this I awakened suddenly in the night to see a leopard looking in the doorway of my cabin. I swear in the moonlight, Monsieur, his teeth looked like the tusks of an elephant. Do not be surprised in the morning when you awaken that you find you have as your bed partner a pretty cobra."

I was roused next day, not by a cobra, but by another

soldier shooting at a crocodile. This crocodile hunting had become the ship's fashion now, like deck tennis on an ocean liner. All day the soldiers were lined up at the rail while the rifles roared as though we were warding off a violent attack of the enemy. I am one of those fussy writers who are a landlord's horror, always complaining about noises in the apartment upstairs and loud radios in the apartment below. I was trying to write a new dispatch and with each new shot I jumped as though I were the target.

The Captain saw me struggling at my typewriter. "Seven days now to Impfondu," he remarked sympathetically. "Then you will have your radio."

We turned into the waters of the Ubangui. Day after day we traveled again in a hazy, trance-like world of trees and birds and crocodiles, suspended somewhere between dream and reality. The river was narrower now, sometimes less than a mile from shore to shore. But the forests grew ever wilder.

A reddish building made of mud bricks showed ahead with a radio aerial on the top.

"It's Impfondu," declared the Captain. "Now you can send your dispatches."

The white-helmeted administrator of the area came hurrying up the gangplank. Eagerly I asked him where I could find the telegraph operator to send my long delayed messages.

His dark face grew troubled. "I am sorry," he said. "The telegraph operator has been stricken with sleeping sickness. Yesterday he became unconscious. There is no one here who can operate the radio."

I should have been prepared for his dismal announcement. For events such as this were a normal occurrence in this strange forest world where the tragic was the usual, and only the pleasant was abnormal.

We stayed at Impfondu a few hours to replenish our wood supply and continued on our way. We had received word at the settlement that the river just above us was falling rapidly; with every mile the water grew shallower. The two leadsmen at the bow were taking soundings constantly.

"M'Sato," called the old leadsman, wrinkled like a coconut. "Three."

"M'Sato," echoed the young Negro, graceful as a tree.

The old man dipped the pole again, and turned to the steersman quickly.

"Moko!" he called in excitement. "Moko! One!"

The young Negro grew excited as well. "Moko!" he echoed.

A moment later there was a dull crashing at the bow. The boat grumbled to a halt. We were grounded on a sandbar.

All day the Captain tried to work the vessel free, using every trick known to steamboat navigators around the world, the washing out of the sand beneath the hull with a hose, the rocking back and forth of the paddlewheel, the endless digging with shovels. Far into the night they labored, to no avail. The vessel was immovable.

We were prisoners of the jungle.

6.
Heart of Darkness

We were marooned in one of the wildest parts of Africa. Ironically the only radio set on board had failed the night before, so that we could not even hear the voices of our fellow men outside, let alone send them any communication. We were cut off from the rest of the world as though we had landed on the moon.

The Captain shrugged his shoulders philosophically. "It's Africa," he said.

I had heard that phrase a thousand times before. I was to hear it a thousand more before the trip was ended.

At dawn a canoe with three ebony paddlers set off up the river bound for Bangui, three hundred miles away, to ask that a smaller steamboat which could navigate this shallow water be sent to our rescue. Whether there was a boat to send, or if sent whether it would ever arrive, no one had the slightest idea.

A crocodile appeared on an island perhaps a quarter of a mile up the river, so enormous when I looked through the Captain's field glasses I could not believe my eyes. The bearded Legionnaire and two other veteran hunters went out in a canoe with their most powerful rifles, and fired a fusillade. They returned soon after, beaming with triumph.

"We have killed him," thundered the Legionnaire sergeant. "Thirty-two feet long he was from his ugly head to the tip of his tail. He was the king of the river, this cochon. Never was there such a crocodile."

He turned to look off in the direction from which he had come, and began to curse violently. The crocodile was crawling calmly onto the bank again, as though no hunter had ever existed.

The Legionnaire and his friends set out once more, and returned, certain this time the monster had been executed.

Half an hour later I saw him lying on the bank, as placid as before.

"He is a lukundu," said the black cook fearfully. "A spirit of evil. They say in the village he is the creature of the witch doctor. When the witch doctor does not like a man or a woman, he tells the crocodile, and that one the crocodile eats."

Several days passed as the glowing sun continued to beat down upon us pitilessly. While I fretted and fumed at this imprisoning Ubangui mud which was keeping me from Leclerc and North Africa. Many times as I saw Alice, a Canadian, wilting in the heat, I reproached myself for not listening to Laurelle and Clapot and taking a plane.

It was perhaps the fourth day of our steaming imprisonment, when there was an unusual commotion down the river. An enormous dugout canoe appeared with a dozen chanting paddlers. In the middle of the craft was a white man, sitting before a child-like individual seeming half his size. The canoe drew alongside and the white man hurried aboard. I needed only one look at him to realize he was Public Health Officer Drussaud, known throughout the jungle as the King Of The Pygmies.

The childlike figure followed a moment later, wearing the red and blue uniform of a French colonial trooper with a scarlet Mohammedan fez set comically on his head; he resembled a dwarf who had put on a soldier's costume to march in a circus parade. I learned he was Manuele, Drussaud's personal pygmy attendant.

Monsieur Drussaud was a towering, big-boned man, as though expressly fashioned by Nature to withstand the rigors of the jungle. He was a famous shot, and the natives of the adjoining village had asked him to hunt down a marauding buffalo who had killed several men within the week. He was going on the hunt, he said, that morning. He invited me to come along.

I abhor hunting animals. But this buffalo was a murderer, who needed to be destroyed.

We set out soon after in Drussaud's canoe, with his dozen black paddlers now chanting a rhythmic war song. I waved to Alice standing on the bow of the steamboat. I felt again the unreality of my life at the moment. It was not true, I said to myself. This was another reel of the Cecil B. De Mille production.

As the canoe sped past the trees tsetse flies came darting at us from every direction. This was an even worse infected area than that through which we had passed a few days before. I was sitting in the center of the canoe, between Monsieur Drussaud and Manuele, the pygmy. As a fly that I could not see lighted on my back, Manuele slapped it expertly; I slapped those on the back of Monsieur Drussaud. No one slapped those on the back of Manuele. He, poor fellow, like most Africans, was compelled to take his chances.

I turned now and then to examine my first pygmy curiously.

"I brought Manuele and some other pygmies down to Brazzaville for an exhibition," remarked Monsieur Drussaud. "They took everything in their stride, the radio, the phonograph, the telephone, the electric light. It was all part of the white man's magic. But the one thing that amazed them was the sight of white children. In this wilderness the only Europeans they had seen were adults; so they thought all white people were born grown up."

Our craft touched the reedy shore. We moved across a clearing, then into a stretch of towering African grass.

Monsieur Drussaud gave me a rifle. "We're getting close," he declared. "The buffalo is the most dangerous game in Africa, and the trickiest. If he appears, Manuele will fire first. If he misses, I will fire. If I miss you fire. If you miss, we all climb a tree."

The pygmy took the lead now, peering ahead cautiously. I followed with Monsieur Drussaud, our rifles at the ready. The buffalo was lurking somewhere in the nearby brush, that was certain from his fresh trail we could see clearly. At any moment he might come charging out with the power of a runaway locomotive, carrying instant death on his giant horns.

There was a crackling as of breaking branches behind a mahogany tree. Manuele halted to listen, taut as the string of an African bow.

Again and again we heard new cracklings and rustlings near us. Each time we raised our rifles tensely, ready to fire.

All afternoon we searched, while the mosquitoes and the gnats and the tsetse flies used my face and legs and arms as a happy feasting ground. The buffalo did not appear.

We gave up the hunt at sunset and started back toward the steamboat. The perpetual green twilight of the forest quickly changed to darkness. Strange animal sounds followed, at times behind us, at times before us, at times seeming to come from all directions at once, screams and wails and laughs and sighs. Far away I thought I heard the trumpeting of an elephant. We stayed closer together now. I was almost walking on Drussaud's heels.

Drussaud peered off into the darkness. "I think there are some pygmies following us," he said. "But even if it were daylight you couldn't see a trace. They're so quiet the other natives think they're invisible."

We arrived at the canoe and set off down the river. Soon the steamboat showed ahead, its lights shining like a cruise boat in some pleasant Mediterranean harbor. We climbed aboard and I counted my tsetse bites. That single day I had been bitten more than a hundred times. Coupled with the many bites I had suffered previously I was acquiring a high percentage in the total of 2500, the average number needed to produce an infection. I was getting very close to winning the grand prize in the lottery. I took my temperature to see if I had a fever, the first sign of the approach of the disease, and smeared some iodine on each bite though I knew it was useless.

Day after day we lay in the middle of the murky river, the boat a furnace which never cooled, with no word of possible rescue.

"Maybe the canoe was lost," said one of the two black boys making up our cabin. "There are many crocodiles. And it is easy to overturn a canoe."

"I think there are no steamboats at Bangui to help us," answered the other. "There is nothing to do but wait till the rains come again in two months and we can go back to Brazzaville."

Our food supplies became exhausted now, as I had feared, and we looked reproachfully at the Viennese surgeon. The Captain sent the deck hands to chop down some palm trees. We lived on the hearts of palm, an appetizing though somewhat monotonous dish, tasting rather like artichokes.

Then late one afternoon twin columns of smoke appeared around a bend of the river upstream. A great shout arose from our weary passengers. It was the steamboat D'Jaa, come down from Bangui at last to take us on our way.

She was a tiny boat, and dilapidated as well, like some of the woebegone steamboats in the last days of the packets on the Mississippi. There were a hundred and eighty of us on the Fondère, and the new boat had microscopic cabins for only six. But we crowded aboard her gleefully, happy as convicts suddenly released from the penitentiary.

Black boys carried the cots of the soldiers across from the Fondère and set them up on the deck of the newly-arrived vessel. When the men had eaten and stretched out to sleep, their mosquito nets were so close together the bodies beneath seemed like curious fish caught in the pockets of a gigantic seine.

In the morning we steamed up the Ubangui, swiftly now, as though the little vessel were anxious to make amends for our long captivity. The country grew grimmer. Often in the villages along the shore the men and women were almost naked. When the men came aboard to help load our firewood, I could see they had the filed teeth of cannibals.

We reached the village of M'Betu, heart of the cannibal country.

"Cannibalism. It is like whisky in your Prohibition," boomed the Legionnaire. "It is forbidden. But still popular. Only two years ago a government man on an inspection trip found human flesh here for sale in the market."

The captain of the D'Jaa nodded eager agreement. "On the last trip of the Fondère at this very spot a passenger became suddenly ill and died. The Captain was compelled to take his body all the way back to Brazzaville, though this took many days. If they had buried him here, he would have been eaten."

It began to rain now, quick tropical thunderstorms with huge raindrops, that borne on raging winds, struck us like bullets from a series of machine guns. Lightning swept the river in great yellow bridges.

A few huts showed at last along the bank, marking the village of Mongumba. An automobile was waiting under some palm trees. It had been sent by the governor of the territory to take us on to Bangui, the capital.

We took seats behind the young native driver.

"You'll never make Fort Lamy," roared the bearded Legionnaire. "With these storms the roads will be like rivers. You should have taken a plane."

The chauffeur was a pleasant youth called Boko, but I was worried from the moment he put his foot on the starter. He was obviously, by Western standards, a very poor driver. I knew that the road we were to take was a mere dirt trail cut through the jungle. It was not the place for amateurs.

In a moment the clearing at Mongumba vanished. The road became a narrow green tunnel winding through the shadowy trees. We sped along two deep ruts, filled to the top with brownish water; each wheel was the center of a dirty Niagara. Soon the hood and the running boards were covered with thick masses of mud. We no longer resembled an automobile. We seemed like some queer-shaped jungle monster floundering down a prehistoric trail.

Every few moments the car went into a skid from which it seemed impossible to recover. I cautioned the driver to go slower. He smiled at me confidently. "Me, Boko, good driver, M'So. Governor say best driver in Bangui. Do not worry, M'So."

A new storm began with the thunder rumbling about us like an earthquake. Boko only drove faster. Suddenly the car gave a terrific leap as though trying to imitate an antelope. An instant later it had left the road and was lying almost on its side in a ditch filled with rushing water. We struggled through the tilted doors with difficulty, and stood in the torrential rain, surveying the disaster.

Boko could offer no suggestion. Night was coming on, with the jungle full of wild beasts—leopards, elephants, and buffalo. As far as I knew it might be days before another traveler might arrive. The situation was desperate.

I had noticed a little hut two or three miles behind us where three black men were working in a patch of manioc. I decided to go back with Boko and try to secure

101

their aid. It was necessary that Alice accompany us, for it was not safe to leave her alone in the car. Elephants were notoriously fond of knocking automobiles about like toys, to say nothing of the other dangers. We set off down the road that was now like a river. In a moment, Alice's fragile sandals, meant for the sidewalks of New York and Hollywood, were sodden lumps of cloth and leather. She went on barefoot, stumbling over stones and sharp pieces of wood. Streams of water were pouring from our clothes; we seemed like a pair of picnickers just rescued from drowning.

Darkness fell. We splashed on, with the aid of my flashlight, watching warily for snakes. The rain stopped and the little hut I had seen appeared soon after. At a few words from Boko the grinning blacks inside caught up crude shovels and axes, and followed us back toward the car. When we reached it I saw the situation was even worse than before. The wheels were up to the hubs in mud, and sinking ever deeper. Boko made a few ineffective attempts at directing the others in getting the car back onto the road. The black men dug and lifted valiantly. But their efforts were vain. We of the West had given the African our tools but had only partially taught him their use. We had given him the automobile. But we had not taught him how to deal with it in trouble.

It is curious how in an emergency the human mind calls upon some distant impression, some long-forgotten bit of information, and summons it to the rescue. Many years before in New York I had seen a film of the French Citroën expedition in Africa, and remembered how those travelers had an automobile accident in a similar area and under similar circumstances. I would have believed all trace of that film would have been obliterated from my mind, so long a time had elapsed since I had seen it, and I had never thought of it since. Now I remembered every detail vividly. I remembered particularly how the men had chopped down small trees and in effect built a little road to get their truck back on the trail. I decided to follow their example. By the feeble rays of the flashlight, I set the men to cutting the saplings and smaller trees growing nearby and laying them down to form a wooden ramp leading to the roadway. The work was accomplished quickly. With relief I saw the car slowly climb the logs and move once more down the road.

Another storm swept us, with a new blinding deluge. The wind rose to a gale. Great branches fell constantly from the trees above us, now and then striking the top of the car like new claps of thunder. Several times immense trees lay in the road, thrown down by the storm. With axes we cut away enough of the branches to let us pass and continued on our troubled way.

Boko gained confidence again and drove faster. Suddenly the car gave a frightful skid, and making a complete circle, turned back in the direction from which we had come. I caught a glimpse of rushing water below. We had skidded on a sort of primitive wooden bridge crossing a little river. One of the wheels had stopped only an inch from the edge. We had escaped falling over by a miracle.

I decided matters could not go on like this any longer. The car was not mine and I did not feel I had the right to replace the driver. But I took the wheel mentally.

"Go into first," I said to Boko, who had become an automaton. "Now go into second. Now back into first. Now second. Now you're all right for a while. You can go into third."

Water began pouring through cracks in the top of the car, and the lights dimmed, probably because of moisture somewhere in the ignition. The windshield wiper grew weaker and weaker. The glass became a steamy blur. We stopped every few minutes while Boko dismounted and wiped the glass with his sleeve.

Some shadows showed ahead in the downpour. They proved to be half a dozen black men, attendants at one of those primitive African ferries known in French as a *bac,* two long narrow planks set on six dugout canoes. We maneuvered the car onto the wooden tracks. The black men took long poles and began to move us across a wide river. We reached the other side and drove on through the stormy night.

Lights suddenly showed ahead. The muddy trail became a paved road, over which our wheels rolled smoothly. Houses began to appear beside us, with shadowy gardens, and army barracks with tall black sentries

104

pacing up and down before dark gateways. I glanced at Alice, drooping in the seat beside me, trying to sleep. I breathed a sigh of relief. We had arrived in Bangui.

We reached the Governor's mansion, but the windows were darkened, for it was three o'clock in the morning. The Governor's guest house adjoining was brilliantly lighted in the faint hope that we still would arrive that night. We went inside and a black soldier quickly set out a simple supper. As far as I was concerned, the most fashionable restaurant in Paris could not have produced its equal.

We revelled in a bath and stretched out on the beautiful white sheets that covered luxurious mattresses. I decided I could ask no more than this even if I went to heaven.

I awakened early with the blowing of a bugle sounding reveille in a nearby army camp.

I looked out the window toward the mist rising in the distance that marked the edge of the jungle. The little settlement was coming to life. More bugles sounded stridently. Soldiers began to stroll down the road in brilliant scarlet uniforms, French officers and black troopers whose figures and faces were a place map of the war in Africa—the small Bantus of the Congo, some not much bigger than the pygmies, the tall Senegalese with scarred cheeks and scarred foreheads, the swarthy Moroccans in flowing robes and sweeping swords as though costumed for a masquerade ball. Overhead an English bomber, probably flown from Nigeria, was circling slowly, preparing to land at a nearby airfield. An armored car rumbled past, followed by half a dozen trucks loaded with munitions. On the blue-painted boxes of shells sat more bright-uniformed black men, calling out jocular salutations to the native passersby. We were getting closer to Colonel Leclerc and the Germans. We were back in a world at war.

A black boy immaculately dressed in white tropicals with a red sash at his waist, appeared hesitantly in the doorway.

"I come from the Governor, M'so. He awaits you and your madam for breakfast."

We hurried over to the building next door, and joining the Governor and his wife, sat down at a tastefully-spread table. The Governor, named Saint-Mart, seemed the best type of colonial administrator, liberal, intelligent. His cultured wife brought an air of Paris to this remote wilderness.

We finished our breakfast and discussed our trip northward.

"He's a genius, this Leclerc," remarked Saint Mart. "And a character. He was only a captain when he arrived in the Tchad and he thought this rank wasn't important enough for the work he had to do, so he made himself a colonel instead. Now the Free French command wants to promote him still higher. But Leclerc won't agree. He says he's not important enough to be a general. He wants to stay a colonel."

An aide came in carrying a large map and pointed out our route.

"There's no problem getting you from here on to Fort Archambault," he said, indicating a dot on the map larger than the others. "But after that nobody knows. You're two weeks late and the rains have already begun. There are no roads, only trails. And you must cross an immense swamp that by now may be impassable. If you're lucky you'll make it. If you're not, you'll be stuck there for months. . . . It's Africa, Monsieur."

There was an even graver problem. The Germans were

moving so fast across the North African coast it was more and more a possibility that Cairo would be captured before we ever arrived. The German victories, moreover, were continuing elsewhere as well. The desperate British were fighting an enemy like the fabled Hydra. When one head was cut off, half a dozen other heads sprang up to take its place. Crete had just been invaded and the British had sent every available man and tank to try to hold this rocky fortress, so vital to their ships in the Mediterranean. At the same time there came intelligence reports of Vichy French aid in Syria to the Iraqui rebels, and of German planes landing in Syrian airfields. There were rumors that Vichy Admiral Darlan had met with Hitler at Berchtesgaden and that Hitler had gained not only the aid of Vichy in the Middle East, but that Hitler had insisted the Vichy troops in Africa open an attack on the Free French territories adjoining. It was likely that at any moment the victorious Germans with their Vichy allies, would start a drive south into the Sahara to seize Fort Lamy and the Congo and split the continent. If they even partially succeeded, with our advance stopped in the North by Rommel's tanks, and our retreat south cut off by the rains, we would be caught in a gigantic trap, and probably spend the rest of the war in a German prison camp.

The aide drove me off to the radio station so that I could send my dispatches. It was a colorful place, this Bangui, where a giraffe might casually wander down a street at the edge of the settlement, or straying elephants, to while away the time, delighted in pulling down the telegraph wires. On the way back from the radio station, we stopped at the single French café and were chatting over a glass of wine, when I saw all the French officers jump from their seats, and seizing chairs or anything handy, begin striking violently at the pavement. An instant later I discovered the reason, a huge green mamba, one of the deadliest of African snakes, who had come up to join the officers for an early apéritif. The snake wriggled off into the grass.

After lunch the Governor took me on a tour of the camps to see the native troops training to fight in the desert. I noticed at once that the men were considerably taller than the short Bantus of the Congo. We were nearing the Sahara now. I was to discover as I went northward that the trees grew smaller and the men grew taller. The pygmies of the jungle gave way to the people called the Saras, with both men and women often over seven feet tall, the giants of the Tchad. A number of them were moving about the streets and markets of Bangui, the men long-robed, with proud, serious faces, the women with finely carved features, and walking like queens. With their royal air, it took little imagination to believe that their ancestors were handmaidens of the Queen of Sheba, who, legend said, had journeyed from the desert to the court of King Solomon.

We made ready to leave forty-eight hours later. A

passenger car was to take us on the first stage of the journey, together with a pickup truck to carry eight or ten black boys and our supplies and bedding.

We drove over for a final chat with the Governor.

"You're going into the lion country now," said his aide with a quizzical smile as he took us to the car. "But don't worry too much. A lion won't attack you unless he's too old and has lost most of his teeth so that he can't hunt other game any more."

I was not much comforted. I wondered if you met a lion, whether you were to ask him to open his mouth and see how many of his teeth were missing.

We had traveled only a few miles from the town when a fierce downpour of rain assailed us.

The face of our driver, a white civilian resident of Bangui, grew troubled. "It is bad, Monsieur," he said. "If it is raining like this to the north, Fort Lamy will be impossible."

The rain ended after an hour. The sun beat down cruelly upon the car as it had on the steamboat; at times it seemed as though we were being struck on the head with red-hot hammers.

The country quickly grew wilder. All traces of the civilization that we had momentarily glimpsed at Bangui vanished. Guinea hens suddenly appeared in the road by the hundreds and then the thousands, so thick we had to slow the car to a crawl to avoid a feathery massacre.

Women clad only in a tu-tu, a few animal tails tied

together, appeared now and then before a hut along the roadside, the tu-tu at times giving way to a banana leaf. After these came natives stark naked, some carrying bows and arrows. They watched us pass in wonder. Occasionally the villages were surrounded by high stockades of wood or straw. I learned they were intended to keep out lions.

The dense forest was gradually thinning, disappearing completely now and then and giving way to grassy savannas.

The car began running hot as we passed a village encircled by hideous masks set on poles to frighten off evil spirits. Near the straw wall a strange figure was standing, a tall man, almost a skeleton. Gay-colored feathers were thrust grotesquely into his unkempt hair. He laughed and talked constantly to himself, now and then executing an odd African jig. He was in the last stages of sleeping sickness, the final hysterical stage that comes before the long sleep. I was grimly reminded of the many numbers I held in the lottery. It would be a few more weeks before I knew if I had won the grand prize.

The driver returned from the village with the water for the car and the chief as well, a wizened old man who brought us a present of the skin of a python, the largest killed in the area for years, over thirty feet long.

We drove on once more.

Darkness descended. I began to worry about our stop for the night. Then a bright light showed in the distance.

As we approached I saw it came from a camp fire in front of a rest house, a large thatched hut built by the colonial government as a shelter for travelers. Some Free French soldiers, all jovial veterans of Africa, had arrived before us and were preparing their supper in an iron pot hung over the flames. Several of them had just fled from the Vichy territories toward which we were heading. We added our supplies to theirs, leaving the cooking to a burly infantryman with a face scarlet as a lobster.

We questioned the soldiers closely. The Vichy pressure was increasing more and more. The guards at the frontier were being strengthened. Escape was growing more and more difficult. Officers and men suspected of sympathy for the Free French were being swiftly removed, and if there was any evidence, carried off to imprisonment or worse. There had been many rumors about the coming of the Germans and a simultaneous Vichy drive to the South. What was going to happen the soldiers did not know.

The usual nightly thunderstorm swept down upon us as we were finishing the meal. We hurried inside the rest-house. A huge lizard lay in one corner of the crude building, moving off sluggishly as we entered. In another corner were half a dozen shadowy creatures with shiny black shells, resembling enormous centipedes. Like the lizard, they crawled off into the darkness.

"They call these rest-houses," rumbled the lobster-faced infantryman. "They are rest-houses for scorpions, and monkeys, and snakes. Anything but a man."

Another soldier with a sweeping blond moustache made a seat of his pack and boomed in jovial agreement, "I am in this same rest house two years ago, my friends. It is dark when I enter and I see a man lying in the shadows asleep. I call out to him, thinking to ask him to join me at my supper. In answer he comes rushing toward me. And then I see it is not a man, but an enormous crocodile."

"Africa is a fight," rumbled the lobster man. "Everything always fights everything else. That is why we old Africans are good Free Frenchmen. Man or beast or insect, we never give up. Even after we are dead. Look."

He found a large black ant perhaps an inch long crawling over the ground, and let it bite his thumb viciously. An instant later he tried to pull it free. The insect would not release its grip. He pulled harder and harder until the straining body at last snapped at the neck and came off in his fingers. The head remained, its jaws still clinging fiercely to the soldier's red thumb.

Soon after the black boys set up our mosquito nets, and we climbed onto our cots. All night I could hear some mysterious creature crackling through the thatch that formed the roof. I hoped it wasn't the mate of the thirty-foot python.

We set off again shortly after sunrise. The road was a brilliant scarlet now, like the red soil of Georgia or New

Mexico. Groups of baboons appeared, watching us with an insolent air, grunting angrily, and hurling after us what were undoubtedly obscene insults. Once we passed a score of monkeys sitting in silence on immense toad-stools, like delinquent children kept after school. Strange birds flew over us such as I had never heard of in the books of naturalists, one with a strip of feathers attached to its body at either side giving it the appearance of three birds flying together, perhaps as a protective gift from Nature to frighten off its enemies. Naked black men sauntered by, wearing a single bushy animal tail behind. It was easy to see where the legends had arisen that this was the fabled land where the men, like the monkeys, had tails.

Toward nightfall we arrived at the village of Bouca. There was a single white man here, a French adminis-trator who had brought his wife, a beautiful Russian, to share his solitude in this wilderness. I first saw her resting gracefully on a divan, with two sleek, green-eyed cats beside her and two tiny mouse deer, scarcely larger than large squirrels at her feet; she seemed the queen of the lost Atlantis.

We had drinks and sat down to dinner. As we ate the two cats watched me with deep suspicion; the mouse deer nuzzled delicately at my ankles.

I found, as the Administrator filled my wine glass that an air of mystery existed here in actuality as well as in my mind. "This is a queer place, Monsieur," he told me.

116

"The natives here believe in child sorcery. Just before my arrival two children had been killed by the tribe because they were said to be terrible lukundus—evil spirits. Only last week another child, a boy of four, was about to be killed for the same reason. The elders declared his guilt was very clear. Each night, they said, he turned himself into a white rat and ate their livers. To save his life I have put him in the hospital. Would you care to talk to him, Monsieur?"

It was arranged that I see the boy in the morning.

After the meal the Administrator escorted us to the guest house, which contrary to the usual custom, lay at a considerable distance from the official residence. As we walked past the queer-shadowed trees which lay between, I was oppressed by a curious ominous feeling, as though the countryside was charged with evil, a mood undoubtedly induced by the grim story of the lukundu. Our spirits were not brightened when we heard that a man-eating lion was on the loose in the neighborhood who within only a few days had killed or wounded a score of natives. It was easy to believe here at Bouca in the ancient legends of certain villages being under a curse.

We reached the guest house, and prepared to retire for the night. The rooms were well furnished, the beds almost as comfortable as those at Bangui. But our windows had no screens and it was too hot to put up the shutters. Our isolation and the open casements were an invitation to the prowling lion. Off in the distance I could hear the

117

beating of drums and a weird shouting and moaning, followed by a shrill voice I imagined was the witch doctor, perhaps finding a new childish lukundu. But I soon fell asleep. I was growing accustomed to the hazards of Africa now. I could sleep like a dog, with one eye and ear open.

After breakfast the Administrator showed me the bleak enclosure surrounded by a few palm trees that served as the public square.

"Now we will see the lukundu," he said.

He sent off messengers in several directions. Soon some stately black men wearing leopard skins had gathered about us, obviously the elders of the tribe. Almost at the same time there appeared a little boy, perhaps four years old, clad in a faded Arab shirt. He stood by himself, facing the Administrator. The black elders regarded him with terror.

I asked one of the leaders, a grave, white-haired figure holding a tasseled spear, to tell me of the trouble.

"O sir, there is great sorrow in the tribe," he answered in melancholy tones. "We have had many terrible lukundus. But never a lukundu like this boy. He is the most terrible of all. Every night he turns himself into a white rat, and eats our livers. I, the chief, have seen this many times and so have many others. I beg you to please speak to the white master here, and ask him to give us back this evil creature he has taken from us, so that we may kill him. For if we do not kill him, soon there will be no men left alive in Bouca. There will be only the lukundu."

At a sign from the Administrator, the boy came closer. I bent over to question him. He was so small his head scarcely came above my waist.

"What do you say of this story?" I asked.

He faced me boldly. "It's true," he answered. "I'm a terrible lukundu. Every night I turn myself into a white rat and eat their livers. I'm going to eat them all."

The story, I am afraid, is without a moral. It is merely another manifestation of the profound mystery which is Africa.

We took to the road again. The country was changing rapidly now, becoming what the English call the Orchard Brush country. Green savannas stretched everywhere to the horizon, dotted here and there with clumps of low trees. Now and then we passed a deserted village, with vultures flying overhead searching for a funereal feast.

We reached Fort Archambault late that night. The Administrator of the area came hurrying to our guest house. "I'm sorry," he apologized. "We must get you off before dawn. The rains have begun above us and the marshes are flooding. It's in the lap of the gods whether you can get through."

We set out just before daybreak, two pickups now, for no ordinary touring car could pass over the road where we would be traveling.

The sun rose fierily. Wide grassy plains stretched into the distance, so smooth, so beautiful, that in my sleepy condition I thought for an instant we were traveling over some carefully-tended millionaire's estate. Herds of animals began to race before us, small antelope with graceful horns and horse antelope, huge as their name; after them came herds of giraffes and zebras and flocks of silly ostriches. Rarely did they travel in groups of twenty or thirty; more often there were two or three hundred. Because of its extraordinary isolation, this was probably the greatest wild-animal area left in the world.

Suddenly some new wild creatures appeared in the distance, as they came nearer becoming a pack of animals about the size of large wolves and looking like hyenas. At the sight the young Negro driver of our pickup grew tense.

The solemn-bearded lieutenant now our escort, who was sitting on a box behind me, reached for his rifle.

"Wild dogs," he said. "We may have some excitement."

The pack raced swiftly across the savanna toward us. I had heard many times of these wild dogs' sinister reputation, how they were dreaded by the natives as much as the buffalo. Many times they had attacked unlucky travelers and literally torn them to pieces. As I watched them dart near to the car, their long teeth bared, ready for the attack, I wondered how these ferocious creatures could be so closely related to our own dogs, so gentle, so faithful to man.

The lieutenant, with his rifle ready, spoke to the driver. The black man put his foot on the accelerator. The car shot forward, with the engine roaring, the horn blowing thunderously. The dogs, in panic, wheeled suddenly and began racing away. One young dog, in his eagerness to escape, skidded on the muddy road, and slid ridiculously on his head and forepaws before regaining his balance. The dogs nearest him, in their mad flight, gave him a look of utter contempt. I could almost hear them saying, "Come on, you awkward fool."

That night we camped in the open. The black boys as usual set up our cots, using long assegais as poles to support the mosquito nets.

The lieutenant looked on with solemn satisfaction. "There are a lot of leopards around," he declared. "But you can sleep soundly. The leopard never attacks anyone under a mosquito net. He's afraid the net is a trap."

Several times during the night I awakened, thinking I heard prowling animals. My suspicions were confirmed in the morning when we saw the footprints where several leopards had circled about us while we slept. But I still am not convinced about the accuracy of the lieutenant's natural history.

As we advanced the villages grew rarer; the road grew worse, then became a boggy trail. Our journey became a series of continuous sinkings in the mud. When one pickup sunk to the hubcaps, the black boys would make a rope fast to the second. The combined power of man and machine would drag the first car forward. New countless herds of giraffes and antelope appeared and huge long-legged birds, standing like grotesque sentinels, clicking their enormous beaks with a sound like chopping wood. It was an animal paradise, an animal garden of Eden.

Another day passed and another. It began to storm again, with flashes of lightning as vivid a red as the earth over which we were traveling. The sogginess of the trail increased. When we went to sleep at night we did not know whether we would be able to go on in the morning.

Our food supplies were running low; the black boys complained of hunger. The solemn-bearded lieutenant decided it was necessary to go hunting. I set off with him just at sunrise, before I left carefully charging the most responsible black boy to look after Alice, sleeping soundly under her mosquito net. In a moment we were deep in the brush, with the camp lost to sight. Strange shapes of animals appeared in the morning mist like phantoms before us, then a beautiful antelope, standing like a statue. The lieutenant fired a single shot. The antelope gave a headlong bound and fell dead. The black boys in triumph picked up the graceful body and started to carry it away. I felt I had assisted not in a hunt, but a murder.

We returned to the camp with the sun still low in the sky. To my horror I saw Alice standing in fright before a giant black man wearing only a leopard skin, and holding an enormous assegai. He seemed a figure torn from the pages of Rider Haggard, a grim, avenging Zambesi warrior out to kill every white man and woman in Africa. Actually he had come from the nearby chief to bring us a chicken.

The trail became only a waterlogged track; on either side wide slimy pools and flooded patches of reeds stretched to the horizon.

The black driver's face became tense again, as when we had encountered the pack of wild dogs.

The lieutenant studied his map.

"It's the last of the big marsh," he said. "If we get through we may be in Fort Lamy tonight. If we don't—"

He shrugged his shoulders eloquently.

The driver gripped the wheel tightly. Mile after mile we slushed and wallowed through the mire. Again and again the wheels went down so deep, it seemed no force could ever dig them free; again and again we emerged and drove stubbornly onward. While the great, long-legged birds stood always watching, clacking their bills as in derision.

Then I saw the driver's tense hands suddenly relax. The lieutenant's solemn-bearded face wreathed in a smile.

"We're across," he said. "We've made it."

We went on swiftly now. Villages began to appear. But their inhabitants were no longer the half-naked men and women we had been seeing for so many days. They were wearing the twisted turbans and the dignified robes of Mohammedans. Once we passed a group of Mohammedan horsemen, and soon after some black Arabs on foot, noisily driving a herd of camels.

We took another ferry and crossed a reddish river. More Arabs appeared, shouting at camels loaded with grain and ammunition, and handsome Mohammedan troopers wearing long, flowing burnooses. Stone buildings showed along the roadside, opening on Arab courtyards like those we had known in Morocco.

"Fort Lamy, m'so," said the black driver happily.

We reached a square that marked the center of the settlement, crowded with camels and donkeys and scribes and soothsayers.

The pickup stopped before a simple stone dwelling.

The lieutenant climbed down from the seat and spoke quietly.

"It's the end of the line," he said. "This is the house of Colonel Leclerc. You've arrived at the Sahara."

8.
D'Artagnan of the Sahara

Leclerc was away inspecting some troops in the desert and would not return until the next morning. His second in command, Colonel Du Pain, a portly figure with the benignant air of a parish priest or a devoted father of a family, took us in charge, and installing us in Leclerc's guest quarters next door, went with us for a stroll about the town.

A troop convoy was moving off to the north in the direction of the territories held by Vichy, now only a hundred and fifty miles away. "There have been rumors of an attack," said Colonel Du Pain. "We don't want to be taken by surprise."

We strolled about the sun-baked streets. It was a fascinating place, this Fort Lamy, where the primitive stone-age cultures of the jungle met the ancient Arab civilizations of the Sahara. Stately Haussa traders in Arab robes bargained with savage black women wearing wide rings in their noses, and an Arab snake charmer played his flute before a swaying cobra. Half-naked black men argued with an Arab magician over the price of a cure for cataract or an infallible love potion. An Arab barber stood shaving a black man whose body was a vivid rainbow of tattooing. Three blind Arab ropemakers wove the piles of hemp before them into long, golden strands, as they worked devoutly chanting verses from the Koran.

It was this colorful settlement which fate had made the advanced base of the Free French forces. A squadron of English bombers, just refueled, was flying off to join in the battle for Libya and Cairo. Fort Lamy was the strategic crossroads, the link that bound Nigeria and the British colonies of West Africa with the Egyptian Sudan and the British colonies of the East. If it fell all Africa would probably be doomed.

Leclerc arrived late in the morning, a slender, wiry individual with blondish hair and constantly-twinkling blue eyes that reflected at once his enthusiasm and gayety. We sat down to lunch in his modest quarters; as I ate a simple but tasty omelet, I thought of the details of his fabulous history. I had learned how when the Germans made their sudden sweep across France and seized his château, he had tricked them into believing he was his own butler, and telling the guards he was going to market, set off on a bicycle through the enemy lines. Soon after he was in England, and then in Lagos, Nigeria, plotting with Miles Clifford, the British Colonial Secretary in that humid African capital, and General Sicé to take the neighboring Vichy-held Cameroons as part of the great conspiracy that brought French Equatorial Africa to the Allies. It was his delight to win battles when the odds were hopeless. He had taken Douala, chief city of the Cameroons, with 24 trusted men; with only 119 soldiers he had seized Koufra far to the north in the Sahara, held by a garrison of 2500.

I am far from a lover of the military. I needed no further convincing after my long experience in the first

128

World War and my briefer experience in this, the second, to know that military combat is the worst of all our many human follies. Yet if the necessity of war ever came again, I decided that if I could choose I would take Leclerc as my companion. For he was not only a soldier, he was a cultivated, delightful human being, blessed with rich imagination and humor. He was a sophisticated D'Artagnan, come to life again in the twentieth century.

A French officer went past the window, followed by a young lion.

Leclerc's blue eyes twinkled again as he saw my astonishment. "You're not in style at Fort Lamy if you don't have a pet leopard or lion."

He signaled the black servant to bring us dessert, and smiled in reminiscence. "I had a pet leopard myself. Till one day I found him on the desk in my office tearing through my papers as if he were looking for some secret document. When he caught sight of me he showed his teeth and snarled horribly, then bolted out the window and raced across the desert, just as if he were a German spy. That was the last I saw of my leopard."

We discussed the grave situation at the Front. Crete had been lost as Alice and I were on the way from Bangui. New fighting had just broken out, this time in Syria, where the British with the aid of the Free French, had moved in to prevent its being taken over by the Germans. But it was an open secret that with British troops fighting on so many fronts, there was scarcely a soldier available for the new battle-line. It would be a miracle if they won a Syrian victory.

Moreover, the assault on Vichy there made it likely that the Vichy territories here in Africa would retaliate by striking immediately at their Free French neighbors. As I had heard on my arrival, there were already rumors of an attack across the nearby frontier.

Leclerc took me on a tour of the camps about the town, where bright-eyed young cadet officers, like those I had seen in Brazzaville, were training squads of tall Saras from the desert. With no supplies and no equipment, Leclerc was preparing to use these troops for a new foray into the wilderness.

That night we visited a makeshift workshop where soldiers after their usual hours had volunteered to repair some worn-out machine guns of a vintage so ancient as to cause any Nazi trooper to burst into laughter. Other volunteers were hammering thin sheets of steel on broken down touring sedans to turn them into flimsy substitutes for armored cars.

As we stood there watching, a swarthy white man approached us timidly. From his dress I recognized him as an Italian prisoner, captured at Koufra. He spoke to my companion quietly.

"Is this work to fight the Germans, colonel?" he asked.

Wondering, Leclerc answered that he was correct.

130

The Italian hesitated. "O sir, we prisoners would like to volunteer, too."

As we strolled about the shop Leclerc's enthusiasm became electric. "I am waiting for the day," he said. "If America ever enters the war or will even send us a few guns and ammunition, I will take my Saras and my camel-troopers all the way to the Mediterranean. We will snip Rommel and his Germans prettily in two."

We remained in Fort Lamy for some time as Leclerc's guest. We became friends, and I learned more and more the rich depth of his character. One instant he would be telling me of some brilliant military stratagem he was planning; the next he would be discussing some French literary classic we both admired. He confided to me his real name—Hautecloque—kept a closely guarded secret. For his wife was in occupied territory. Had the Germans known her husband was the daring French officer who with his raids was so undermining the morale of their Italian allies, she would have become a hostage beyond price.

Often Alice and I ate with the fatherly Colonel Du Pain and his staff in a room overlooking the Shari River that flowed into Lake Tchad a few miles beyond. The room was large, but the heat of the sun, reflected through the open windows, made us seem as though we were under the concentrated rays of a burning glass, about to be set on fire.

In a recess of the wall a tiny, scarlet-turbaned black

boy sat pulling at an enormous punkah, suspended from the ceiling directly over the long dining table. The movement of the punkah varied exactly with the attention of the French officers sitting beneath. When the officers grew absorbed in discussion, the punkah would swing slower and slower, then stop altogether. The head of the tiny black boy would droop lower and lower; his eyes under the scarlet turban would close sleepily.

Suddenly one of the officers, on the verge of suffocation, would realize what had happened. He would roar out "Punkah!" The tiny black figure would waken with a start that almost sent him tumbling from his perch. The great fan would move back and forth frantically.

All day along the banks of the river we could see the crocodiles crawling sluggishly and the hippopotami wallowing in the sun. It was a mysterious stream, this Shari, flowing into the even more mysterious Lake Tchad. Though we traveled the lake's shores for several weeks, I never saw it even once. It was a dying lake, constantly shrinking in a drying-up cycle of the Sahara. Aviators told me they had seen a large expanse of water in the center. But this was something I was compelled to take purely on faith. As far as my own eyes could tell me, Lake Tchad was only an endless marsh, with immense flocks of strange, long-legged water birds stalking through reeds twice as tall as a man.

Our permanent escort was a clean-shaven, cheerful young lieutenant named Lamy, like the town—I suspect the name was false. Appropriately he owned a half-grown pet lion, who for some reason found great charm in my presence. Whenever I came to his master's quarters, he would start a noisy purring that sounded like a volcano on the verge of eruption, and throw his paws around me with deep affection. I would stand there frozen, trying not to shiver, torn between pride in having aroused this devotion in the king of beasts and abject terror.

I talked to the English representative of the Speers Mission. There was again no hint of the volcanic explosion that was to occur a few months later in Syria, an explosion so violent its ashes, like Krakatoa, would sweep across the world.

The rumors of an attack from the Vichy African territories increased. No one knew from moment to moment where or how the onslaught might come. As the rumors grew ever stronger I became anxious to visit the camel troops guarding the frontier, Leclerc's pride and joy, and again see if I could learn what was happening for myself.

We set out for the Vichy border before daylight one morning, wakened by a knock of our black caretaker, and breakfasting hastily, went outside to find the energetic Lieutenant Lamy already waiting. Our destination was a desolate region called Tibesti, one of the most remote parts of the continent, where there was no definite trail, only the track of camel caravans. Few even of the

French military had ever visited the area; apart from its vital military significance, this would be turning a fascinating new page of my book with the padded cover.

I examined the vehicles for our journey with curiosity, like our expedition from Fort Archambault, consisting of two pickups, one for ourselves, one full of black soldiers who were our escorts in case of an attack. In addition we carried long strips of canvas and sheets of tin to make a road when we went down in the sand—and as important as our bullets, a number of gasolene tins filled with water. Before our problem in the rain forest and the swamps beyond had been too much moisture; now it was not enough.

Colonel Du Pain came to see us off. He checked the rifles and the ammunition with Lieutenant Lamy, then inspected the water supply, hidden under a tarpaulin to protect it from the sun. He added two more cans for safety.

"You can survive without most things in the desert, *chers enfants*," he said in his fatherly tones. "But even a camel cannot go without water. Save it to the last drop."

A moment later we were speeding down the road. We stopped briefly at the microscopic military radio station with the usual antenna showing above the roof. We went inside.

"Tell them we are starting," said the lieutenant to the solemn soldier sitting before the instrument board. "Two pickups at six hours, zero four. Two pickups. Monsieur

134

and Madame Burman, Second Lieutenant Lamy. Eleven tiralleurs. Send it in code. They are watching our communications. I don't want our American friends to send their dispatches from a Vichy prison."

The operator began to click out the message to Mao, the distant desert fortress toward which we would first be traveling. If in four days we did not arrive search parties would start out in both directions.

We hurried through the door and set off in the car again. For a few short miles a narrow road stretched before us, soon becoming two deep ruts in a yellowish plain, devoid of any vegetation.

A compass was fixed to the wheel before our black, scarlet-fezzed driver. I noticed that the lieutenant's alert eyes followed its slightest jerky movement.

"They always say driving in the Sahara is like sailing a ship at sea," he remarked. "Only on the ocean, the old timers tell me, you're allowed to make a few mistakes. In the desert you can't make one."

The empty yellow plain soon changed and began to resemble the arid regions of Old Mexico, wide stretches of sand and clay dotted here and there with patches of cactus and groves of tall palmetto trees. The parallel ruts that served as our guide disappeared; there was now no sign of a track, only the occasional prints of the padded feet of a camel.

A cloud of dust appeared in the distance, when we neared it becoming a caravan of heavy-laden camels tak-

135

ing supplies up to the front. The camel was the chief means of transportation here; our car was a rarity.

Swiftly we drove past the plodding animals and their black, grunting drivers. The caravan became a new cloud of dust and vanished behind us.

A lone zebra appeared soon after and crossed in front of the pickup, then a whole striped herd, racing in wild panic. Beautiful birds flew over us again in dazzling arcs, and more ungainly, spindly-legged birds resembling storks stood motionless, watching as we passed, like distrustful sentinels.

Suddenly the car jerked to a halt. The engine began to labor; the wheels ground noisily. There came that sickly sweet smell dreaded by every desert driver, the smell of burning rubber as a spinning tire grates against sand.

"Looks like we're stuck," announced Lieutenant Lamy.

We climbed out hurriedly, to find the wheels sunk deep in powdery sand. Quickly at the Lieutenant's direction the black soldiers in the pickup behind took a strip of canvas and spread it under the wheels. Soon we were under way again.

The sun mounted higher in the sky. Alice and I began to grow thirsty. We emptied our canteens, then filled them from one of the metal tins in the back of the pickup. Despite the tarpaulin with which it was covered the water seemed as hot as if we were boiling it for coffee.

The day advanced and the sun beating down upon the barren plain seemed to have even greater intensity than on our journey farther to the south. I was so hot it seemed impossible I did not have a fever. I knew if I were so affected it was as nothing compared to what Alice was suffering. We arranged a box as a seat for her in the middle of the pickup. The bumps were worse but the heat a little more endurable.

There came a new grinding of wheels under the pickup and a new smell of burning rubber. Lieutenant Lamy jumped out and cursed under his breath. All four wheels were well over their hubs now. We had fallen into a sand trap that appeared to have no bottom.

The black soldiers laid a new road, this time of canvas and sheets of tin, stretching before us perhaps forty feet. I had thought before leaving Fort Lamy that our precautions were somewhat unusual. Now I only hoped we had been careful enough.

The soldiers began to dig out the sand swiftly with long shovels. As they worked a family of white-robed Arabs, a man, wife and three children suddenly came from nowhere and stood beside us, watching in silent curiosity. We were in the midst of a desolate wilderness, with the nearest village many miles away, yet at once we had this audience. It was an instance of a mysterious, unexplained phenomenon familiar to every Sahara traveler. Stop a car anywhere in the wildest desert; in five minutes an Arab appears.

Soon we were free of the sand again and rolling onward. All day the dreary, perspiring cycle continued, a sudden halt, a smell of burning rubber, a spreading of canvas and tin.

A trio of black Arabs mounted on beautiful horses rode toward us from a clump of palmetto, and hailing the pickup, asked for water. A hyena or other animal had destroyed their goatskin bags the day before, and neither they nor their horses had drunk since. We gave them enough to slacken the thirst of both men and animals, even at the risk of our own supply. For this is the first law of the desert; as long as the traveler has a drop of water he must share it with those in greater need.

It grew late. The lieutenant studied his map and began to watch the cloudless horizon intently. His usual cheerfulness had given way to anxiety.

"We should be coming to a village where we can spend the night," he said. "I hope we haven't lost our way."

We drove on for several miles. Still no sign of habitation appeared, only the cactus and the tall palmetto, casting longer and longer shadows as the sun dropped lower in the sky.

The lieutenant mentioned the name of the village to the driver and pointed to the map.

The driver nodded. "Gone, gone," he said cryptically.

The lieutenant did not understand.

"Gone, gone," the driver repeated. He drove on a short distance and looked about as though trying to find some landmark, then sped on toward a grove of palmetto

138

forming a wide circle in the distance. He reached the outer fringe of trees, and driving past, suddenly halted. Before us were a score of recently-abandoned huts already thickly overgrown with brush. It was the village we were seeking, deserted by its inhabitants because of some plague or sudden disaster.

We continued onward. Toward dusk a group of other native huts, shaped like immense beehives fifteen feet high, were silhouetted on the top of a shadowy ridge.

We left the pickups at the base of the elevation, a fixed sanddune covered with patches of coarse grass, and climbed toward the settlement. A black man in Arab dress came forward to meet us, a gracious, magnificent figure like the Saras, over seven feet tall.

Lieutenant Lamy spoke to him a moment in the native dialect, then turned to us with satisfaction. "This is the Sultan of the village. He says he'll move out of his palace with his nine wives so you and your lady may sleep in peace."

We followed him to a beehive hut somewhat larger than the others, and were presented to nine black women, as tall and stately as the sultan himself. As darkness fell they moved into the adjoining dwelling, leaving Alice and myself in solitary splendor. The black boys carried in our cots, and began to cook supper.

We ate, and quickly crawled into bed. We were still in the heart of the lion country. Off in the distance we could hear the great beasts roaring like faint thunder. But we were too exhausted by the long trip across the desert to listen, and soon fell asleep.

I awakened with an intolerable burning of my skin, as though I had been dipped in a vat of gasoline and then set afire. I looked across at Alice, and by the moonlight streaming into the hut, saw that she was sitting up in bed, obviously in the same painful condition. We were both being attacked by some frightful, invisible kind of flea, another of the ingenious inventions contrived by Nature to keep this section of the vast continent an unexplored wilderness. The torture was too great to bear.

Reluctant to disturb our generous hosts we decided to seek refuge down below in the pickups. The lions were roaring loudly now, and seemed to have come much closer. We resolved to go on to the cars nevertheless. For in Africa the traveler soon becomes a realist, who lives for the day and the moment. The fleas were certain torture; the lions only a possibility. And even if the lions came, by comparison to these devilish insects we felt we would regard them as friends.

Quietly we made our way down the sandy ridge so as not to wake the sultan and his bevy of wives sleeping in the neighboring hut. The two pickups were parked close together beside a clump of towering cactus. Quickly we made beds of the cushions in the front seats. When Alice was curled up comfortably in one, I closed the door, and stretched out in the other.

We fell asleep with the roaring of the lions in our ears.

9.
Camel Corps

We resumed our journey at daybreak. More fixed grass-covered dunes appeared; the pickups rolled between them steadily, as the tires for the moment found a hardened trail. A herd of ostriches galloped ridiculously before us, then a snow-white antelope, the almost mythical Ariel. Now and then a graceful gazelle would stand motionless and watch us pass, curious about these sputtering animals of which it had no experience.

The fixed dunes grew fewer now, becoming varied with hills of drifting yellow sand.

The lieutenant studied the horizon with youthful eagerness. "This is mysterious country where we're heading. I've heard stories that if you go far enough you can find blond men who are descendants of the Crusaders. They're supposed to have traveled along the Mediterranean on their way from the Holy Land, and then been pushed back here into the desert. The rumor goes they have crucifixes tattooed on their arms and their wives are the most beautiful women in the world."

He gave an order to the driver to shift direction slightly, then went on talking. "Queer thing happened a little while back. An army friend of mine on a mission here heard of one of these Crusaders, blond and blue-eyed and married to a princess with golden hair. My friend went out to look for him and found him after weeks of searching. He turned out to be a German who had

THE GENERALS WEAR CORK HATS

deserted from the Foreign Legion, and was married to the daughter of a Mohammedan chief, black as coal."

The sky ahead darkened suddenly. A great yellowish cloud, as though a distant forest were on fire, appeared and moved swiftly toward us. It was a sandstorm, sweeping down the Sahara. A fierce wind began to blow with a violence that set the pickup to shivering oddly. The air grew thick as with a smoky fog. The sand began to beat against the windshield and the metal roof with a noise like rattling dice. The sharp grains struck our faces as though someone were hurling at us thousands of tiny, invisible tacks.

"We'll have to stop," said Lieutenant Lamy.

We halted with our accompanying pickup beside a patch of cactus, and buttoned down the canvas curtains. I sat looking out into the whirling obscurity. I had seen sandstorms in the Sahara before, when they had continued three days. But then I had been safely lodged in a pleasant, palm-fringed oasis, not in this bleak wilderness. I hoped this storm would not last so long.

For several hours we sat, waiting patiently, while the drifting sand continued its steady tattoo. We grew hungry and tried to eat some bread and cheese we had brought from Fort Lamy. Our mouths were so full of grit, it seemed as if we were eating sandpaper.

Suddenly the storm ended. The murky fog vanished. The sun reappeared in a molten sky and beat down upon

144

us with renewed fury. We brushed the sand from our clothes and faces and drove on.

We camped in the open at nightfall, and went on again at sunrise. The last fixed dune soon disappeared behind us. There were now only immense swells of sand, stretching off endlessly to the horizon. A slight breeze was blowing. The sand, drifting off the tops, crowned each dune with a tiny rainbow, like the waves on a bright, windy day at sea.

Suddenly a white stone tower showed in the distance over the top of a dune, then some massive stone walls pierced in the center with a high-arched gateway. We had arrived at Mao.

At regular intervals in the walls small cannon were visible. Below these were barbed-wire entanglements and concrete tank traps intended to halt any invaders. In the tower a lookout was standing, watching the horizon where the Vichy territory lay for any sign of an approaching enemy.

The heavy wooden gates protecting the entrance were shut, and a black sentry, standing outside with fixed bayonet, challenged our car. Lieutenant Lamy showed our papers. The gate opened ponderously; we drove inside. It was as though we had stepped upon a stage set for an Arabian Nights opera. About us were perhaps forty or fifty sleek camels, with gorgeous scarlet tassels dangling from their heads and tails. Standing beside them were black men in red fezzes and tunics and baggy red trousers. Other soldiers similarly dressed were marching up and down, raising and lowering their rifles at the curt command of a burly sergeant.

The illusion of an Arabian opera was further heightened when two white men, obviously officers, came forward wearing scarlet blouses and Turkish pantaloons, looking exactly like actors intended to represent Haroun-al-Rashid and his chief Wazir. I would not have been at all surprised to hear them suddenly burst into song. They were followed first by a pet deer and then by a young ostrich, striding comically over the sand. The designer of these fantastic costumes for the desert troops must have been possessed of a profound sense of humor. For these soldiers of the Camel Corps were among the toughest fighters in the world.

The two officers greeted us warmly, the major, who was the commandant, a breezy vivacious Southerner, his adjutant a quiet Parisian. The major gave us his quarters, a simple stone-walled room hung with beautiful Arab draperies. We lunched on excellent macaroni, captured by Leclerc from the Italians at Koufra. I heard first-hand how spies were reporting much activity in Vichy territory. The garrison was in instant readiness for an attack, however it might arrive.

It was easy, I learned, to send out spies in this area. For here there were no border posts with guards and prying immigration men; here there were only dunes and white-shrouded Bedouins with faces all alike, who recognized no frontiers. When necessary one of the officers would dye his face and arms and put on an Arab robe. Pretending to be a date merchant or a dealer in salt, he would join a passing caravan bound for Vichy territory and Zinder or Timbuctoo.

As a result of its location, this fortress was a haven for the Free Frenchmen escaping from Algeria and the North; here they would rest after their tormented voyage across the Sahara, and then continue on to Fort Lamy. This was the point where came the melancholy news of those who would never arrive, but had died of heat and thirst in the desert.

The major and his adjutant spoke sadly of their fellow officers only a few miles away who had chosen the Vichy side, some of whom had been their close associates. Here the war was different than in other parts of the world; here it was profoundly touched with the personal. Like our own Civil War, it was brother against brother.

To my astonishment, some time after lunch, I heard a bugle blowing reveille.

"It's the second reveille," explained the major in the genial accents of his native South. "This is the reveille from the siesta."

We walked about the fort. Some black soldiers were firing with machine guns at a toy airplane, sliding back and forth on a wire.

Suddenly the bugle sounded shrilly. Soldiers darted off in various directions to man concealed anti-aircraft

147

guns; others seized the tethers of the camels and rushed them off to stone shelters built inside the walls. The ostrich, trained to the signal, rushed after the soldiers, its wings flapping, its neck stretched out absurdly, and jumped into its own shelter near the entrance.

"Just a practice alert," said the Parisian dryly. "We want to be ready for the real one when it comes. Even the ostrich."

The alarm was soon over. As the men resumed their normal activities, I saw that one of them, supervising a drill, was carrying an alarm clock.

The major chuckled. "We can't get any watches," he said. "But we happened to have a few old alarm clocks. So when we need to know the time we carry a clock instead."

We went off to the neighboring village, a collection of beehive huts like that we had abandoned for the lions. This was ostrich country now. The inhabitants, tall men and women related to the Saras, lived chiefly on ostrich eggs and ate off dishes made of the shells, cut in half. Ostrich eggs decorated the top of every hut, put there to bring the dwellers inside good fortune.

We returned to our quarters. Some grinning black prisoners from the military barracks, sentenced for some minor infraction of the military code, entered the room carrying great buckets of water, and emptied them into a barrel standing in what passed for our bathroom. We splashed some dipperfuls over our hot bodies and felt refreshed.

"I'll wake you at five tomorrow," announced the major amiably as we finished a pleasant dinner. "When I heard you were on the way I invited all the chiefs in this area for breakfast. They'll be coming from over a hundred miles. I'm afraid, my friend, you'll have to make a speech."

I was roused before dawn by the clatter of hoofs, and the piping of flutes. As it grew lighter I could see Arab chiefs in gorgeous costumes arriving on beautiful horses and camels, their saddles covered with jewels and fine-wrought silver and gold. Occasionally one of them would be preceded by musicians like those who had waked me, shrilly playing flutes or Arab bagpipes.

Alice and I dressed hastily, and went to the main hall of the fortress. A long Arab cloth was spread over the bricked floor. Around it were sitting forty or fifty Arab chiefs, some obviously white, some ranging in color from the faintest tinge of brown to the usual mirror-like ebony. At their head was sitting a wrinkled Arab with a trailing white beard. Before him lay a whole roast sheep.

The bearded Arab made a long speech, ending with a prayer that the Allies would win the war.

The major leaned toward me. "They don't like the Italians for what they did to the Arabs in Libya," he said. "And they know the Germans would be worse."

The other chiefs joined in the prayer piously.

149

The commandant leaned toward me again. "It's your turn now," he whispered.

I stood up dazedly. Accustomed to writing far into the night and rising accordingly, my brain does not begin to function until noon. My watch showed five minutes of six. I was still six hours from normal. Moreover, making a speech at any hour was difficult enough. To make a speech in French at dawn was nothing short of appalling. My ambassadorial chickens had come home to roost.

I made the speech, though of what I said I haven't the faintest idea. Something probably, as when I had spoken to the cadets in Brazzaville, about loyalty to friends and freedom and courage and the usual platitudes a good ambassador is supposed to utter on such occasions. My limping French seemed to give the guests pleasure. The bearded Arab broke off the first piece of meat with his fingers and handed it to me with ceremony. The feast had begun.

It ended with drinking three kinds of tea and chewing cola beans. We went outside for an Arab fantasia, one of those exhibitions of fancy Arab riding so familiar to anyone who has ever watched a newsreel from Algeria or Morocco, showing a reception for a visiting Sultan. We took our places at the end of a long enclosure, and I reminded Alice what was going to happen, how the Arabs on their magnificent horses would come sweeping madly toward us, pulling up their mounts only at the last second. I cautioned her no matter how terrified she might be, not to flinch. The reputation of the Ambassador's wife and the Ambassador and all Western culture was at stake.

A moment later the horses came charging down upon us, the taut riders emitting terrifying cries like the screaming of an attacking horde of animals. They reached us, and death seemed certain for us both under the wildly plunging hoofs. Then suddenly the forelegs of the horses nearest us jerked high into the air as their riders strained at the bridles; the upraised hoofs seemed to miss our faces only by inches. I looked at Alice and saw she was standing stiff as a statue. The reputation of the Ambassador and the West was secure.

I left Alice next morning in the care of the two gay-robed officers. Mao, however fascinating, was only a means to an end. My destination was the farthest camel patrol guarding the Vichy frontier, the eyes and ears and first line of defense of Free French Africa. We had only one pickup now. Lieutenant Lamy, with a grizzled French sergeant who was to be our guide and driver, carefully checked the fuel and water supply. The car was bristling with rifles and a machine gun, ready for instant action. We would soon be within gunshot of the enemy.

We drove off to the primitive radio station as we had done at Fort Lamy to advise the commandant ahead of our coming, and set off across the yellow sea of dunes. The sergeant, a desert veteran, watched the color and texture of the sand every instant. At times he would send the pickup racing headlong down a dune and onto the shallow beyond. At times he would put it into low gear and let it climb laboriously to the top, as a truck climbs a steep mountain. Our journey became an intensified repetition of the days before, constant sinkings into the sand and going forward again with strips of canvas and tin.

Mirages showed ahead, great lakes with palm trees growing alongside. Occasionally the illusion was so intense our wheels were almost in the imaginary water before it vanished. Then at the base of an enormous dune a gay-tasseled camel appeared and another and another, soon becoming a whole company of camels, tethered in the sun. We had arrived at the patrol.

It was like a new scene in the Arabian Nights operetta. Atop the dune were pitched a score of tents, like the temporary settlements of the Bedouins I had known in the Northern Sahara. In the middle was an elaborate tent made of beautiful Arab rugs stretched on poles, obviously the headquarters of the commander. An Arab camel-trooper stood as a sentry nearby, looking out over the enemy territory stretching below him, a rolling waste of dunes each topped with its faint sandy rainbow. Not far away other Arab troopers were moving about, carrying water or brushing their camels' sleek hides. Here and there a lean soldier was stretched out sleeping where he could find a bit of shade, blissfully ignoring the activities of his red-turbaned companions.

The driver brought the car to a stop before the tent made of the fine-woven rugs. From it there emerged a figure who at first sight appeared to be one of the officers we had left behind at Mao, suddenly transported here by the jinns of some Arab magician. His blouse was the same flaming scarlet; his flowing pantaloons could have been worn appropriately by the Sultan Haroun-al-Rashid. Even his gay spirit as he greeted us was like that of the jovial Mao commandant. Like the other he was from the South of France, where a light-hearted nature is proverbial.

A beautiful dog resembling a collie followed closely at his heels. The officer, a captain, introduced the animal merrily. "I call him Fifth Column," he said. "It keeps me reminded of what's happened in France."

The dog, unaware of his guilty name, wagged his tail blithely.

The captain was ecstatic at our visit. We were the first persons from the outside world he had seen for many months. It was an incredibly lonely life, this life of the camel trooper, the méhariste. But anyone like myself who loved the desert knew that I was talking to a happy man. He was a Leclerc on a smaller scale, another D'Artagnan who would have been miserable engaged in the ordinary pursuits of mankind. His world was the scorching wind and the ever-shifting dunes, the swaying camels and the crescent moon and stars, full of poetry and beauty.

The captain turned to me jovially. "You'll have to review my troops," he said.

A bugle sounded. The troopers, on their camels now, paraded before me, racing their ungainly beasts in choking clouds of dust, and firing their rifles wildly as they charged.

Suddenly the sun above me seemed to become an enormous fireworks pinwheel, spinning dizzily for some extraordinary Fourth of July celebration. The camels and the turbaned soldiers joined like riders around the outer edges and began to whirl madly against the blinding sky.

I turned to the scarlet-robed captain beside me. "I'm afraid I'm going to faint," I said.

An instant later I dropped limply to the ground. For perhaps five minutes I lay there, never quite losing consciousness, while the captain stood over me, splashing water in my face. I arose a little weak and somewhat ashamed. A Southerner accustomed to heat, I had gone about for weeks under the sun of the jungles to the south with impunity. It made me realize the fierce intensity of this sun of Tibesti in the Sahara, which these Frenchmen and natives must bear.

The review began again. By the time it ended I was completely recovered. The captain was taking a patrol to reconnoiter the vague, imaginary line which marked the enemy territory. He invited me to come along.

154

He led the way to a group of camels kneeling nearby, and moved to the side of a magnificent animal, grunting to itself, that was to be my mount.

"Take off your shoes, my friend," he said. "We méharistes always ride barefoot."

I realized why as I climbed into the saddle and put my feet against the beast's furry sides. We in the West have almost forgotten we possess heels and toes; to the camel-trooper they are as vital as his bridle.

I had barely settled myself in the saddle when I saw the camels near me suddenly rise up and start racing across the desert. An instant later, I felt myself propelled into the air as though I had been shot from a gun, and my camel swiftly followed the others. I had often ridden camels in the deserts of Algeria and the oases of Morocco. But this riding a mehari was in a different world, a different universe. It was as riding a worn-out old nag harnessed to a junk cart is to riding a race horse in the Derby. I swayed from side to side like a fishing boat in a North Atlantic storm holding on for dear life to the wooden pinion at the front of my saddle, certain with each new pitch or roll that I would go hurtling to the sand.

For an hour we traveled along the rolling dunes, the camels trudging slowly now as the captain riding close beside me, studied the horizon.

"Look's like all's quiet," he said. His gay southern face grew serious. "We've had a Vichy plane flying over the last few days. Something's going on. I don't know what.

We can handle the Vichy French. If the Germans come it won't be too easy. It's hard to stop a tank with a pen-knife."

We returned to the camp.

It was easy to see the deep devotion of these soldiers to the merry captain. This war in the desert was a personal war. What counted was the men who were the leaders, not the causes.

The captain arranged a dance of the troops. As the drums began to play the soldiers swayed back and forth in frenzy, occasionally leaping high in the air like Russian Cossacks.

It grew dark, and we sat down by the flickering light of an acetylene lamp to eat an antelope stew. Near us the drums continued their steady throbbing as the soldiers continued their impassioned dancing.

Suddenly a hairy shadow raced out of the darkness, seeming as large as the china plate on the sand before me. It was a huge tarantula, common in the desert area. Soon there was an invasion of tarantulas, probably attracted by the glare of the lamp. One of them raced across my bare leg, and another followed in quick succession. But oddly they made no attempt to bite. As a tenderfoot I received great credit for coolness and courage. Actually I did not move because I was paralyzed with terror. But it did my reputation as an ambassador no harm.

The hairy invasion ended. The captain clapped his

hands in signal to the Arab soldier acting as cook over the open fire.

He turned to me, his face glowing with impish delight. "I will show you we camel men are not barbarians," he said. "I have prepared for you that consummation of the divine art of the pastry cook. It is a baba made with rum."

He clapped his hands again. A black soldier came forward carrying the baba on a tray and set it before us. It was an exquisite baba, far better than many I had eaten in my penurious days on a side street of the Left Bank of Paris, near the Boulevard Saint-Michel. How he managed to find the ingredients for a baba here in this bleak wilderness, and even more taught his cook how to make it with no more than a few rocks as a stove and some desert brush as firewood is still one of the unsolved mysteries of the war.

The gay meal was over at last. A soldier made my bed for the night, a simple matter of scooping out a hollow the length and width of a human body, with a pile of sand at the head for a pillow. I put my blanket in the depression, and stretched out awkwardly. On one side of me lay Lieutenant Lamy, on the other the captain, with Fifth Column curled up peacefully at his feet. A short distance away I could see the soldiers still at their dancing, punctuating their movements from time to time with curious noises, like the barking of dogs. They were like automatons now, remaining always in the same spot, as though they were mechanical soldiers dancing on top of eight-day clocks.

I lay there wakeful, listening to the sounds of the desert, the weird laugh of the hyenas, the queer bark of the jackals as though mocking the dancers. There came the curious sound of two large birds fighting, the angry beating of wings, the clashing of bills, like men battling with sticks. An anvil bird sounded its single sonorous note, as though calling for peace. Overhead the stars shone like nickeled bits of metal.

Several times I arose and tried to smooth the sand beneath my blanket, to make my bed a little less uncomfortable. Each time the captain would raise his head instantly, ready to assist. His sleep was like that of a watchful desert animal, ever alert for an approaching enemy. Now and then he bolted to his feet when a sentry, pacing up and down nearby, made an unusual crackling sound as he put a few sticks of wood on the dying fire.

I slept until I was wakened by the sun beating down upon my face. The captain escorted me to a tent where a soldier was sitting beside a primitive radio.

The telegraph key began to click noisily. "Calling Mao. Calling Mao. Pickup returning 5 hours, 58. 5 hours, 58. Acknowledge."

We walked back to the pickup where Lieutenant Lamy and the grizzled sergeant were waiting. I climbed into the seat.

158

The captain waved goodbye. "Sorry about the baba," he called. "Too stuffy. I'll make a better one when you come again."

We sped down the dune, and the tents and the gay-tasseled camels vanished. I was touched with deep sadness as one is touched on leaving something beautiful he knows he will never see again.

I returned to Mao and soon after with Alice was back in Fort Lamy. It seemed impossible that the disasters in the wartime world outside could continue, but there had been more black days in our absence. The British, attempting to fight their way out of the German noose pulling ever tighter about their garrison at Tobruk, had been repulsed with tragic losses. With their newly-won bases in the Mediterranean, the Germans were bombing the Suez Canal mercilessly. Moreover in the wake of all these victories word had come that Egyptian politicians, encouraged by the British losses, were swinging openly to the side of the Nazis. It was daily becoming more and more likely that if we delayed much longer in taking off for Cairo our hosts there would be Hitler's army.

Only in Syria were the Allies making any advances. I decided to go there at once.

We made our arrangements with the Speers Mission to leave on the first plane available for Egypt, where we could make our way to Damascus and the other battle-fields of the newly-developed war, and crawled into our beds that night, happy at the prospect of a few undisturbed hours of rest. We were sound asleep, when I was awakened by a thunderous knocking on the door. I tossed off the thin sheet covering me and dashed across the room to answer, not knowing whether it was an air raid or an attack from the desert. I opened the door quickly. To my amazement I saw Colonel Du Pain standing there, his broad, fatherly face tense with excitement.

"There's terrific news," he said. "Just come over the radio. Hitler has invaded Russia."

I grabbed Alice in her nightgown, and like Hitler after the fall of Paris, danced a jig with joy. Then more dignified, we made the colonel come in and have a celebration drink. England and this infinitesimal remnant of France were no longer alone.

A day later we bade Colonel Du Pain and Leclerc goodbye.

Leclerc shook my hand. "Come with me the day I enter Paris," he said with a smile.

I was happy to promise that I would.

It was a promise I failed to keep.

We drove with our baggage to the military airport. A plane appeared as scheduled overhead; to our dismay it showed no sign of stopping. Somewhere a military clerk or radio operator had made a mistake on one of his numerous papers and forgotten to instruct the pilot to come down.

Another aircraft appeared not long after. When the control officer signaled the pilot to land, it turned out to be a cargo plane rushing some special, badly-needed ammunition to the firing line. Some boxes marked "High Explosive—Handle With Great Care" were moved over to make room for us on two of the crude bucket seats in the cabin. But with our extra weight the plane was loaded to capacity. We could not take an ounce of luggage, not even a toothbrush. Sadly we said farewell to our mountain of suitcases piled on the dusty ramp, and climbed into our places.

The propellors roared. The plane soared over the desert. The scene of the melodrama in which we were participating was to shift now from the Sahara to Egypt and the Holy Land and the deserts of Syria and Arabia. A new act, an act laid in the mysterious Middle East was about to begin.

III.
ARABIAN
NIGHTS

10.
The Waters of Damascus

Fort Lamy became some scattered stone huts in the hazy distance. A caravan showed beneath us, a score of heavy-laden camels winding slowly over the reddened earth. The caravan vanished. There was only the desert and a giant red dust whirl, believed by the natives to be a wandering jinn.

The red earth changed into a desolate waste of sand, like that we had crossed on the way to Tibesti. The plane rocked as in a violent storm; the boxes of explosive began to dance alarmingly. I wondered just how much of a shock it would take to set them off and blow us all into space. The bounding of the plane grew even more violent. In my ignorance I had thought that traveling over a desert would be the smoothest kind of flying; I was to learn that it was almost the worst. The shadows cast by the dunes and the rock ridges create wide differences in temperatures and air pressures, causing the struggling propellors to falter and flounder.

A mountain rose before us, streaked in different tones of red as though it were made of Christmas candy. Suddenly the plane gave a convulsive leap forward, then dropped like an elevator broken loose from its cables. I shot upward, crashing my head into the ceiling of the cabin. The boxes of explosive danced up with me a few inches, then came down again to the cabin floor with a noise like heavy artillery.

Down the plane plunged, faster and faster, then when

165

perhaps eight hundred feet above the earth, came out of its dive and roared onward. I dashed over to see how Alice was faring. A more careful traveler than myself, she had kept her seat belt fastened, and was sitting calmly, still holding the magazine she had been reading. I dabbed a handkerchief against a slight cut in my forehead, our only casualty, and looked in wonder at the boxes of ammunition now scattered topsy-turvy about the cabin. The pilot, coming in to investigate, told us we had hit an air pocket and dropped vertically 1500 feet. Why the explosive did not blow up is a riddle I still cannot solve.

We came down at El Facher, a dismal airfield and barracks in the middle of the Sahara, sharing our room with the most horrible spiders I have ever seen, huge creatures whose legs and bodies seemed to be covered with a shiny shell-like substance of sickly pink so that they resembled badly-boiled crabs. Late in the afternoon next day we sighted a city built at the junction of two rivers flowing out of the desert. It was Khartoum, at the junction of the Blue and White Nile.

We had dinner in a palatial hotel, and took a bath, our first real wash since leaving Lisbon. I looked about our room with its elaborate draperies and rich-upholstered furniture, and thought of our lives the few months previous. The contrast was incredible. I realized now why man instead of the cockroach or some other tenacious insect ruled the earth. Man was more adaptable. One minute we had been in Brazzaville, steaming like a pudding, the next we had been in an open airplane, freezing at 12,000 feet, the next we had been back on the ground, a steaming pudding once more. From a steamboat crowded with 180 people though there were staterooms for only six we had gone to backbreaking pickups, and traveled hundreds of miles across roadless plains and deserts. We had endured crocodiles, tsetse flies, heat, sandstorms and everything that hostile tropical nature could offer. No self-respecting cockroach could have survived.

Morning brought a huge Sunderland flying boat. We set off northward over the Nile. For two days we flew with the river ever beneath us, a glassy thread of water bordered by twin strips of green that marked the irrigated areas, and beyond that a sandy chaos stretching off to infinity. Then as if by magic a vast city appeared, stretching for miles across the sand, with lofty domes and minarets, and now and then a stately avenue like those of a beautiful European capital, the Arabian Nights with a touch of Paris. Beyond we could see the great Pyramids and the lonely Sphinx.

We came down at an airfield. White-robed Egyptian porters rushed at us, screaming for our luggage, though we had none, having abandoned it with our hopes at Fort Lamy. Other figures, red-capped like the vultures of the desert, swooped down like the birds they resembled, offering to change our money. Beggars tugged at our clothes, insistently demanding alms.

167

I heard a voice call my name, and to my delight saw the friendly face of Brian Guinness, come to the airport to meet us. A moment later we were climbing inside a cab. The driver, holding the door open to let my wife pass, leaned over to me confidentially. "You want some dirty postcards, Sidi?"

We were in Cairo at last.

We drove through the streets at breakneck speed. The signs of war were now everywhere. Anti-aircraft batteries, surrounded by sandbags, showed at strategic street corners, and armored cars and tanks rumbled noisily. The sidewalks were crowded with Allied soldiers: grinning British Tommies and tall Australians; South Africans with wide brimmed hats and Free French Africans in the scarlet-striped uniforms of Zouaves. Open trucks moved past, full of unshaven soldiers just come in from the front at Tobruk and other trucks full of neat shaven men on the way to take their places. Intermingled with them were all the strange races of this fantastic Middle East where our civilization was born; richly-turbaned men from Saudi Arabia, followed by their silken-clad wives, shrouded in veils; long-bearded men from Yemen, looking at the wonders about them with unbelieving eyes; black men from Ethiopia with long thin faces that might have been taken from the carvings of an ancient Egyptian tomb.

Our cab halted in front of the Continental Hotel where we planned to stop, for we had heard Shepherds was a marble mausoleum; a traveler, our friends had said, would feel more at home in the Taj Mahal.

The taxi driver gave me a leering wink, and pressed a bit of pasteboard into my hand. "Maybe you want pretty girls, Sidi. My name on the card. Just call Yussef, Sidi."

Within an hour we were installed in unaccustomed luxury, and having dinner with Brian Guinness and the other members of the Speers Mission at a sidewalk table of a swank restaurant. There was supposed to be a blackout. Actually it was a blue-tinted obscurity that gave every passerby the appearance of a corpse. Now and then a bluish magician would halt beside our table, and turn a handkerchief into a white rabbit, or pretend to break an egg in a Speers Mission hat and take out a baby chicken.

To celebrate our safe arrival we went off to a cabaret. It was crowded with British soldiers in from the fighting at Tobruk, celebrating like ourselves. They were a jolly crew, laughing and joking constantly. The Germans might arrive in Cairo any minute, or they might be killed at Tobruk tomorrow. But they were brave men who long ago had learned how to accept the hazards of war.

The air in the cabaret was so thick with tobacco smoke an airfield weather report would have said visibility was zero. On a shabby stage a belly dancer was twisting and writhing grotesquely, her fat body decorated in strategic areas with a few ten-cent store diamonds. Before her a half-dozen sweating Egyptians in shirt sleeves were beating drums or droning out a monotonous Oriental tune on battered lutes and guitars. Suddenly an air-raid siren outside wailed shrilly. The lights went out, leaving the room in smoky blackness, broken only where a laughing soldier struck a match and applied it to a cigarette. Now and then there came the sound of a voice in a rich Cockney accent damning the Germans, and occasionally the answering feminine giggle of some non-Cockney but highly appreciative partner.

I went to the door and looked outside, curious to see if this, my first air raid since my arrival in Africa, differed from those I had experienced so often in the first World War. Great searchlights swept the black sky, trying to find the German planes I could hear buzzing overhead. Machine guns went rat-a-tat-tat on every street corner as anti-aircraft cannon boomed in irregular accompaniment. Tracer bullets left a weird glowworm-like trail; Very lights dropped in signal from the British fighters overhead, like fireworks for some gala holiday. It was extraordinary how nothing had changed from the first world conflict. The planes flew a little faster, the guns shot a little farther, that was all.

The searchlights began to swing off toward the west. The clatter of the machine guns and the booming of the anti-aircraft cannon lessened as the German planes sped off to the desert bases from which they had come. The all-clear sounded and the lights flashed on. The belly dancer recommenced her giddy gyrations.

For several days I stayed in Cairo with more air-raid alarms and long talks with British and Free French officials as I prepared to go up to the Front. From various sources I heard that the Vichy lobby in America had redoubled its efforts. But the facts revealed in my dispatches could not be denied. I was gratified to learn they had now swung the body of public opinion solidly behind the Free French. Long a director of the Authors League, I was a friend of many prominent authors and journalists who knew that I had no axe to grind. As a consequence the Vichy propaganda intended to influence those writers was an almost total failure.

The policy of the American government, on the contrary, was if anything even more pro-Vichy. I had made many new friends. But I had made some powerful enemies. As a result I found that my position was changing rapidly. I was losing my job as Ambassador without portfolio from America to the Free French. I was now rather Ambassador without portfolio from the Free French to America. Fortunately, thanks to Paramount Pictures, and my dispatches, my bank account was still holding out.

I had a long talk with Alexander Kirk, the American minister to Egypt. He impressed me as the usual product of political diplomatic appointments, a rich man probably excellent at golf and cocktail parties, but not possessed of the penetrating mind needed to deal with the devious intricacies of Egyptian and Arab politics. But even he, on the spot, could see what was happening and had the good judgment to disagree sharply with the policies of the government he was representing.

"Keep telling them the facts," he said as I was leaving. "Maybe Washington will be convinced in the end."

I am nothing if not an enthusiast. I decided to intensify my fire on the Vichy hierarchy.

Cairo itself was incredible, a bizarre chapter out of a preposterous mystery novel. I was in British uniform now, complete with Sam Browne belt and desert blouse and shorts. To the ordinary eye, I was a British officer. When I sat down in the lobby of the hotel, scarcely five minutes would pass before a ravishingly beautiful girl would take a seat beside me and drop her handkerchief, or engage in some other hallowed trick of the female spy, practiced since the days of the wars between Rome and Carthage. So numerous were these exotic Mata Haris, so obvious their performances, that one of our favorite recreations was to pick out the spies from the innocents.

The realistic British recognized the facts. On the walls of the hotel were large posters with the caption usual in wartime at the top, "Don't Talk—A Word May Mean A Thousand Lives." Directly underneath would be a picture of a kindly English lady, with the admonition, "Don't Tell Mother." Below was an elderly English gentleman beside the advice, "You'd better not tell even

Father." And at the bottom, in enormous letters, "Above all, don't tell this one," beside the picture of a beautiful naked girl, holding out her arms.

The notorious attraction of soldiers to women was apparent even in the local dictionaries. An oily figure waiting in the street inveigled me into buying a supposed English-Egyptian phrase book. I turned to the first page, beyond the feebly printed title "Egypt Language necessary for Britis Troops. What Every Britis Troops should know." I read the opening paragraph with its carefully translated Egyptian equivalent:

Good morning, Miss.

I love you, Miss.

Would you like to go for a walk?

Are you a prostitute, Miss?

How much?

I went off with a British official to the fashionable Gezira Club for lunch to conclude my preparations. Around us were the colorful uniforms of regiments that had made British history, the Black Watch, the Coldstream Guards, the Cherry Pickers.

"We're sending you up to the Syrian Front as a Distinguished Personality," said my host with a twinkle in his eye, as he motioned the waiter to bring me another gimlet, a drink popular with Anglo-Egyptian diplomacy. "Major Bell will be your personal escort. That way you can go anywhere you please. If you went as a regular correspondent you'd be rather limited."

173

I smiled as I thought of myself in the first World War, a buck private rear rank, sleeping in a stifling bunk far below the waterline on a troop transport going to France, or cleaning out sewers and latrines in some muddy camp set in the middle of a swamp. Being an ambassador was much better.

We drove to the British Embassy where the official had his stately office, and talked of the Syrian campaign and certain highly secret details of what would be the Free French participation. Now and then my companion made notes on several sheets of paper. It came time for me to go. The official put the notes in a metal tray resting on his desk for the purpose, and struck a match. He watched until the last scrap had burned to ashes.

"This is Cairo," he said cryptically. "If I left these on my desk they would be in the hands of the Germans tonight."

A few hours later Alice and I packed our bags, which by a miracle had arrived at last from Fort Lamy, and eating a hurried dinner, were joined by Major Bell, who told us a cab was waiting.

I looked with relief at his deep-tanned, friendly face and listened with pleasure to his warm, Kentish voice, as I knew we would be together for some days. Any war is bad enough. It is a hundred times worse with an unsympathetic companion.

We went out to the taxi.

"Yallah," said the Major to the shabby-fezzed driver. "Let's go."

We drove down the crowded street, on our way to the Holy Land at war.

Past trolley cars dimly glowing with the same bluish haze of the street lamps overhead we made our way, past horsedrawn carriages full of noisy British soldiers. We reached the railroad station where half a dozen comic trains, caricatures of those we know in America, were waiting beyond the iron gates, their locomotives hissing fiercely, their bells ringing with a clamor as though to rouse all Cairo for a terrible flood of the Nile. We found the train for Jerusalem, and pushing our way through a mass of Egyptians waiting for no apparent reason on the platform, climbed aboard a dingy coach. The train was already packed to the windows with British soldiers. Rifles and ammunition belts and blanket rolls and water bottles were piled on the baggage racks and the floor, or hung perilously from hooks in the walls.

Somehow we managed to squeeze inside. A soldier with an incredible Cockney accent gave Alice his seat. Major Bell and I prepared to stand all the way to Jerusalem, our first stop. It was a merry train, noisy with soldiers' jokes and lusty humor about the girls they had left behind them.

For an hour we waited inside the coach, like badly-packed sardines. The train had been due to start as we came aboard. There was still no faint sign of its moving. It was early July, and the summer winds were sweeping like blasts from a battery of blowtorches off the desert. Even the locomotive had now ceased its alarmed

175

clanging, as though it, too, had abandoned all hope. Major Bell and I went outside and walked forward to the engine where an impatient crowd of soldiers was gathered. The fat Egyptian engineer poked his sweating head out the cab window.

"Yallah!" called one of the soldiers. "When are we starting?"

The engineer shrugged his fat shoulders. His face had a curious, enigmatic expression, fatalism, knowledge, cynicism, a combination of the wisdom of the Pyramids and the mystery of the Sphinx.

"Inshallah," he answered. "Allah will decide."

For another hour the train stood there motionless. Suddenly the engineer began to jerk the bell furiously and shouted at us some words of Egyptian I could not understand. We scrambled wildly aboard. The soldiers in our coach gave a derisive cheer. The train pulled slowly out of the station.

Noisily it rattled over the tracks, the engine puffing laboriously as though afflicted with some strange respiratory disease. Soon Cairo with its beggars and its mosques and its raucous bazaars was behind us. Some Australian soldiers a few seats ahead began to sing a cowboy song. "Yip Yipee!" they chanted. Some of the other soldiers joined in the refrain.

We rolled on for perhaps half an hour and pulled into another station where more troops were waiting. The sardines inside squeezed tighter to make way for the new sardines climbing aboard.

The train showed no sign of leaving again, as though once halted, it was unable to regain its momentum. We all bolted outside once more. Half a dozen steaming trains were halted on sidings nearby, like ourselves, paralyzed.

A British army captain searched the sky anxiously for German planes. He spoke to an Egyptian railroad official standing near.

"My God, can't you get some of these trains out of here before they all get blown up?" he demanded.

The official smiled oilily. "Inshallah," he said, like the engineer. "Allah will provide."

Despite his smile, in his voice there was an ill-concealed hostility. In my innocence, before leaving America I had believed that the Egyptians were allies of the British. I had quickly learned that many, if not most of the official class would be happy if the Germans arrived.

At last the train began to move again. New shadowy stations drifted past, and more sardines waiting with packs and rifles.

Suddenly a huge circle of lights showed ahead, blinding in the blackout. I learned it was a camp for Italian prisoners, illuminated in this fashion by the British so the helpless captives would not be annihilated by the bombs of their German allies, come to raid the nearby Suez Canal.

The Canal itself showed ahead, a narrow strip of water touched faintly with the reflection of the stars shining overhead. It gave no hint of its vital importance in the war. At regular intervals along the banks anti-aircraft guns were starkly silhouetted against the sky, so effective the planes of the enemy had blocked the Canal only once, and then only for three days.

We reached the water's edge, and scrambling out of the train hurried aboard a ferry. The awkward craft lumbered slowly to the other side. We were at Quantara, the beginning of the Palestinian railroad to Jerusalem. A shadowy depot showed ahead and a shed of the Palestine customs. The blackout was intense now. We groped our way to a train waiting nearby, found Alice a seat, and hurried off to the station to buy sandwiches and coffee. After more groping in the darkness, we found the door to the restaurant and had just given our orders when there was a terrific explosion outside. It was an air raid with no advance warning. This junction of the two railroads and the Canal was a favorite spot of the Germans; they were raiding here around the clock.

We snatched our sandwiches from the counter and rushed back to the train to look after Alice. We had numerous alarms in Cairo, but this was Alice's first real attack. We found her sitting calmly in the compartment where we had left her, protesting mildly to the Arab guard who was putting iron shutters over the windows. She was not concerned about the raid. But she was greatly worried that the shutters would give her claustrophobia.

At once the great searchlights streaked through the sky and the anti-aircraft batteries began a steady thunder. Above the roar of the guns came the droning of the enemy planes, like evil, stubborn mosquitoes.

I discovered that night the way to make a Middle Eastern train go fast; it is to arrange an air raid. We were not scheduled to leave for at least another hour. But with a despairing shriek of the whistle, like an animal in its death agony, the train fled into the desert. Madly it sped as more bombs dropped nearby, leaving behind a dancing trail of sparks and flame like a newborn comet. A train, running on a track, is a perfect target. It is as helpless against an airplane as a rabbit is against a tiger.

As we raced along I had time to think of this Syrian battlefield where I would shortly arrive and its tragic meaning if the battle were lost. I had learned in Cairo its full significance, how its failure would mean the loss of Suez and perhaps the loss of the war. And I had learned the details of the Vichy treachery which had made this new war necessary. In nearby Iraq a high Iraqui official in the pay of the Germans had started a revolt against the British-Iraqui alliance. The Vichy governor of French-held Syria had given the Iraqi rebels badly-needed guns and ammunition. Even worse, in secret he had permitted German planes to use Syrian airports; intelligence reports showed that the Vichy officers, drinking Hitler toasts, were preparing to turn over all of Syria to the Nazi armies. To the British such a move would be fatal. For Syria was part of the narrow land bridge connecting Africa and Europe and Southern Asia. Across this bridge lay all the supply routes linking these three continents. It was for the possession of this bridge that armies had fought since before the dawn of history. Without this bridge and without Suez not only the western Mediterranean, now under hostile control, but the eastern Mediterranean as well would become a German sea.

The British, fighting with their backs to the wall, struck before the Syrian span of the bridge could be turned over to the enemy. Their men and equipment were pitifully few, some scattered British and Australians and South Africans and a small number of Free Frenchmen. Whether they would win or lose was now in the lap of the gods.

The train gave a final lurch forward as the last bomb dropped into the starry desert. The attack was over. The train began to wind through the dark Palestine hills. The sky brightened with the first touch of dawn. The train began to halt frequently now, dropping off groups of British soldiers. At each stop Arab children came aboard, to sell us beautiful Palestinian oranges.

The train stopped at Lydda where a military car was waiting. We climbed in behind the driver, and set off for Jerusalem. Through the hills where Jesus had wandered we sped, whirling around dizzy curves resembling corkscrews gone mad. Then the Holy City appeared, the new town with its modern buildings of creamy stone, the old city with its Tower of David rising like a desert fortress above the ancient wall.

Through the streets of the new town we drove swiftly, everywhere passing shrouded guns and half-tracks and tanks. The land of the Prince of Peace was an armed camp.

I left Alice at the luxurious King David Hotel, for she could accompany me no farther at the moment, and with Major Bell climbed into an army truck loaded with soldiers bound for the firing line.

Around more giddy curves we wound, and up and down hills and jagged mountains. Nablus showed ahead, and Nazareth, the home of Jesus. A bomber was circling overhead. We were not sure whether it was friend or enemy. We rumbled down a steep mountain and saw the Sea of Galilee stretched out before us, blue as the cap of the Free French Blue Devil riding with the British soldiers in the back of the truck. A fishing boat with a beautiful colored sail was coming into shore, with some weatherbeaten fishermen standing in the bow, just as Christ might have stood two thousand years ago, back from a trip with his fishermen disciples.

We reached the Syrian frontier, the usually busy customs shed bleak now, deserted. We passed by quickly.

181

Great shell holes and larger bomb craters began to appear in the road before us. In the ditches alongside lay burned trucks and tanks, and the broken shell of an airplane. The burned tanks and trucks became more frequent, then some wrecked armored cars and artillery. There had been a heavy battle here. The ghosts of the guns and the tanks became rumbling reality as we drew nearer the fighting line. Convoys passed us, heavy cannon with caissons full of ammunition, Bren carriers, tanks crawling like turtles, and half-tracks crawling like lizards. Here and there a convoy would halt for a brief rest. With lightning swiftness the anti-aircraft gunners unlimbered their weapons and pointed the glistening barrels to the sky. Some black Free French troops passed in a truck. From their faces and their insignia I could tell they were from the Tchad. I called to them in French. They grinned and waved excitedly in answer.

The mountains near Damascus came into view, touched with snow even though it was midsummer, then a great Mohammedan city again with gleaming mosque domes and lofty minarets. It was Cham, the ancient of the ancients, Damascus, already old when the Bible was young. The sun set as we reached the gardens that marked the suburbs. The road was jammed with military traffic now and our pace was slowed to a crawl. It was almost night when we moved down the Street Called Straight. Off in the distance we could hear the rat-tat-tat of machine guns, and the heavier rumble of artillery.

A battle was going on somewhere beyond the city. At every street intersection troops sat beside machine guns, in case of the return of the enemy driven out some days before. Ambulances sped past, carrying the wounded off to the hospitals. Through the growing darkness white-robed Arabs moved like ghosts.

The rumble of artillery in the distance grew louder, as though the battle were intensifying.

We had arrived at the Syrian War.

If one of the fortune tellers I had seen in the market place at Cairo had told me how I was to be involved in its climax I would have told him that he had gone mad.

11.
Scheherazade

We found a shabby hotel still open despite the battle, and climbing a dreary flight of stairs to a room with a shattered window, went to the officers' mess just started in what might have been a restaurant.

The Syrian waiters with infinite politeness brought us yogurt white as the snow-capped mountains nearby and stuffed vine leaves and the red wine of Damascus. Shortly before with the same politeness they had been bringing the same food to our enemies.

We returned to our dingy quarters to sleep. I awakened with the melancholy cry of the muezzin, calling from a nearby mosque. "Allah. Ou Akbar. Mahomet, Rasoula, Illala," he chanted, so that the waiting Faithful could bow in prayer.

The chattering of the machine guns beyond the gates formed a weird accompaniment.

After breakfast I made a brief visit to the Free French troops holding the line a few miles beyond the town. Among them were some jolly Circassian soldiers whose ancestors had been transplanted here from their home in the Caucasus Mountains by their Turkish conquerors many years before. I remembered with a smile a dispatch I had seen in Cairo when a certain Colonel Colette had escaped from Vichy territory in Syria, bringing with him some tough native fighting men, "Colonel Flees With 500 Circassians." I had always thought Circassians were beautiful girls.

185

I lunched with General Catroux, commander of the Free French forces in the area. He was a quiet man with a sensitive, thoughtful face, who looked as though rather than a general he might be the president of a great university. They were a remarkable group, most of these Free French rebel officers, men who were deep thinkers and humanitarians first, and soldiers afterward.

In the streets and the bazaars the life of the city went on much as usual, the lemonade sellers with their great-spouted brass containers, like Russian samovars, the soothsayers, willing to tell who would win the war for a penny, the veiled young women walking along with a withered crone and watching sometimes nervously, sometimes flirtatiously every young man that passed.

I made my way back to the hotel. On the wall opposite a soldier was pasting up a huge poster.

I read its grim warning in French. "Attention! Anyone aiding the enemy will be shot."

In the evening we dined with the wife of General Speers, head of the Speers Mission, now my official sponsor at the front. General Speers was away for the moment. His wife, who graciously did the honors in his absence was Mary Borden, the British novelist, who had come to Syria with her husband and started a field hospital to care for the wounded. She was happy to see a fellow author in this strange city so far from the literary chit-chat and the garden parties of London.

We were joined by some bluff colonels with sandy

moustaches and Scottish accents so thick they seemed caricatures invented by some English humorist to fill up an odd page of *Punch*. I almost needed an interpreter. They were followed by some beautiful, aristocratic English girls acting as nurses in the hospital. The conversation seemed partly out of a Kipling story, partly from a modern British play of West End society. General Speers arrived when we were at the table, a British businessman turned officer, whose enthusiasm for the Free French was only equalled by my own. He was more than cordial.

The days passed quickly and the sputtering of the machine guns and the rumble of artillery lessened as the fighting drifted farther and farther from the town. I busied myself with my dispatches, visiting the front and talking with the Free French soldiers and officers or the devil-may-care Australians who made up so large a part of the British forces. At night I had more dinners with Mrs. Speers and the beautiful nurses and the Scotch colonels I could not understand.

After dinner one night I stopped at a crowded Syrian café. Red-fezzed and turbaned Arabs were sitting at low tables drinking tiny cups of coffee, while peddlers moved among them in cajoling voices, as they tried to sell the gaudy rugs or cheap nylon stockings draped over their arms. Some jaded musicians, sweating in their shirt sleeves, played whining violins and squeaky flutes; on a platform before them a fat belly dancer writhed absurdly as she cast longing glances at her sometimes bored, sometimes entranced audience. It was Cairo all over.

In the café was a placard, like the poster I had seen earlier, warning that a firing squad would be the penalty for anyone helping the Vichyites or the Germans. I had already heard that spies were as common here as in the Egyptian capital, and quiet assassination even easier. The death of a political enemy could be quickly arranged for any reasonable price. A city in the Middle East seems to have been especially designed by Providence for spies and intrigue. The high walls, the arched doorways, are full of mystery; the Arab costume itself, which can so quickly veil a face or hide a striking knife is perfect for espionage and murder.

Major Bell, having seen me fairly established, set off in a car going back to Cairo. I abandoned the dreary room with the shattered window and moved to the grand hotel of the city, more fitting for an ambassador.

And then there again reached out the long arm of coincidence, in a way so preposterous that it could be found only in the pages of a fiction writer who had lost all honor. In this hotel was also quartered a character almost legendary in Syria, the exotic Princess Atrach, the Emira of the mysterious people called the Druse who lived off in the remote fastnesses of the Druse Mountains. Their little-known customs and religious practices differed sharply from the Mohammedans by whom they were surrounded; rumor said they still worshiped in strange rites the ancient goddess Astarte.

188

They could be a fierce as well as a mysterious people, these Druse over whom the Emira ruled, as the French had earlier learned to their sorrow. Fifteen years before, they had revolted against the French emissaries governing their territory and crushed with frightful casualities a force sent against them ten times their number. The Princess, I was informed, had lately swung the powerful Druse army single-handed to the side of the British; if the Allies won the Syrian war much of it would be her personal victory.

I happened to meet the Emira one day, and she invited me to have coffee. As I looked at her delicate face and her almost almond-shaped green eyes peering out from under long black lashes, I saw at once that she deserved her reputation as a famous beauty. Small and exquisitely formed, as she walked to a table her rhythmic step and graceful movements gave the instant impression of a dancer. When I saw her a little later come sweeping in splendor down the grand staircase of the hotel, she was a princess in effect, as well as reality, a figure out of a Franz Lehar operetta, or better a modern Scheherazade. I was not surprised to learn, that amazingly for a high-born woman of the Middle East, she had once acted for the films in Cairo.

We met a number of times afterward, and chatted about the war and politics and Western culture in which she professed much interest. She invited me at length to visit herself and her husband, the Emir, at their residence in the Druse capital, the mystic and once forbidden city

called Es Soueida. I little dreamed that invitation was
the beginning of the most dramatic episode of my life, an
episode that made me a witness and participant in an
event that reached far across the Mediterranean to De
Gaulle and Churchill in London, with startling consequences in the war.

I continued to encounter the beautiful princess, and
each time she gently renewed the invitation. I was careful each time to find a logical and polite excuse. Having
lived in North Africa for a considerable period, I was
familiar with Arab intrigues that go far beyond the
purposes apparent to Western eyes. I thought I knew
the reason for the proferred hospitality. But remember-
ing all the stories I had read in the Arabian Nights of
scimitars and men being drawn and quartered and
dragged behind the Sultan's swift white horses, I did not
care to learn that my guess was wrong, and wake up in
Es Soueida with a dagger in my ribs.

The British and the Free French troops fought valiantly against the Vichy regiments. The ambulances
rolled steadily through the streets. The fighting beyond
the city turned sharply in the Allies' favor.

An officer coming up from Jerusalem brought me
word that Alice was fretting in the costly luxury of the
King David Hotel; she begged to be allowed to join me
at the Front. Through Mrs. Speers I arranged the permission, and making a quick trip to the Holy City,
brought her to Damascus.

She had been with me only a few days, making sketches of the troops, when an excited rumor swept through the city as a grassfire sweeps the prairie. The rumor said the Vichy French were surrendering, and there would be an armistice. I made a hurried trip to headquarters and to my joy found the rumor to be true.

The cease-fire went into effect shortly after. That night there was great gaiety in Damascus among the Allied soldiers. Everywhere Australians, British, and South Africans and Free Frenchmen moved up and down the streets, laughing and joking, arm in arm, and when they could, drinking large amounts of whiskey and beer and wine and anything liquid Damascus would provide. There had not been many Allied victories to celebrate.

And now I fell into an adventure of a kind that comes occasionally in the grim melodrama that is war, a bit of pure farce comedy. As part of the cease-fire, the Allied troops at a certain hour were to move into the city of Beirut, the busy seaport of the then united Syria and Lebanon, called by some the Paris of the Middle East. I was anxious to witness the occupation, the fruits of the bitter fighting here, and hurried over to see General Catroux. From him I learned that the bulk of the Allied troops would be moving north to the city along the coastal highway from the British bases in Palestine. I asked for permission to make the journey by the shorter mountain road over which I had traveled in peacetime

191

many years before. The General quickly agreed, and said he would send a car.

We breakfasted early next morning, and I went out to buy somè food for the journey, for on such a trip it was impossible to know when next we would eat, and I was aware of Alice's idiosyncrasies. Delicate in physique as she was, with the faint appetite of the proverbial bird, she nevertheless insisted on her canary seeds at quite regular intervals. She went with me anywhere on one condition; I must keep her fed.

To my dismay as I left the hotel I found the shops were not yet open. After much inquiry I found one at last, a tiny confectionery selling only the crystallized fruit for which Damascus has long been famous, probably since the Middle Ages. Crystallized fruit was not exactly the perfect diet to last through perhaps several days of the Occupation. But since there was nothing else I bought an enormous bagful, hoping that in an emergency it would at least support life.

The car called for us soon after, to my surprise a handsome civilian touring car driven by a chauffeur wearing a red tarbouche and a suit of European clothes, which looked as if they had been slept in all night. I learned that all the Free French military vehicles were going by another route. This was a car specially hired by headquarters from a garage for our journey.

As the hotel boys piled our baggage into the rear the driver was arguing at the top of his lungs with a white-robed figure sitting beside him, who I had learned was the vehicle's owner.

"I do not wish to go," he shouted and moaned, waving his hands wildly. "I have been talking with the soldiers. They say this road it will be full of mines left there by the Vichy troops and the Germans. I have a wife and seven children. I have also an old father and mother. What will happen if I am blown high in the air? So?"

He made a frantic gesture of being blown to pieces.

The face of the white-robed owner was swept with agony. "You are a madman," he shouted in answer. "Always I have known you are mad. And I am mad also because I have continued to be your employer."

The driver jumped out of the car, screaming insults. The owner followed. They stood there berating each other, so violently a crowd of Arabs quickly gathered.

I was anxious to leave and stepping into the argument reminded the driver that Allah watched over his Faithful. "Kismet," I said. "What will be will be."

The Arab bystanders added their opinions.

"The Sidi is right," said a gray-haired old man in a snow-white turban. "What will be will be."

The driver raised his hands to Heaven, then to the white-robed owner again. "You have brothers. You have cousins. Why do you not let them drive this car?"

The owner seemed about to explode with apoplexy. "I will pay you double," he screamed.

The expression of the driver suddenly changed. He made a supreme gesture of resignation.

"Kismet," he said. "As Allah wills." He jumped into the car again.

Alice and I climbed in hurriedly beside him before he could change his mind. The driver's face became that of a man walking to the electric chair. He hesitated as if about to leap outside again, then seizing the wheel, put his foot on the accelerator, and tooting the horn like a wounded elephant, sent the car hurtling down the crowded street. Wildly he drove, missing donkeys and Arab carts and lemonade sellers by inches, and followed by a rain of curses sufficient to damn him and his seven children and their children's children to eternity. Through more swarming streets he sped, in a nerve-shattering frenzy. At times he would see someone he knew standing on the sidewalk. He would bring the car to a violent stop that sent us crashing against the windshield, and leaping out, would hold a frantic discussion whether he should make the trip. A moment later he would jump back to the wheel and drive on again insanely. I have had many crazy drivers in my wanderings, in Paris, in Algiers, in Belgrade, in Baghdad. But never have I had the equal of that Mad Demon of Damascus.

The streets were filled with rumbling tanks and rattling Bren carriers and sputtering protection trucks, their anti-aircraft guns ready for action. We drove past swiftly.

We reached the village of Dimas some twelve or thirteen miles from Damascus, where I had been a few days before during some heavy fighting. A long line of military vehicles was waiting here, shrouded with fishnet camouflage flapping in the wind. A roadblock showed ahead. The driver's swarthy face grew pale. He brought the car to a sudden halt. A solemn British soldier came up and asked to see my pass. He took it to a tall, statuesque colonel of the Black Watch standing beside a camouflaged staff car.

The Colonel read it and strode toward us.

"Can we get through to Beirut?" I asked.

The Colonel answered in flawless Oxford accents. "I'm afraid not quite," he said. "The road ahead is full of mines. It's my job to pick them up. We move at ten when the armistice goes into effect. I suggest you wait here and we'll open up the road together."

He produced a bottle of whisky. For perhaps an hour we sat there in the shade of a barren yellow mountain, chatting and drinking Scotch, now and then munching a bit of Alice's candied fruit.

The time passed quickly.

The colonel consulted his watch. "Ten o'clock," he said. "Time to be moving." He spoke to an aide, then turned to me again. "The engineer car will go first to pick up anything dirty that's out there, and I'll come after. Tell your driver to follow me."

Our chauffeur, who had been sitting peacefully during the interval, wrung his hands when I passed on the Colonel's instructions. "I do not wish to go," he pleaded despairingly. "My wife. My seven children."

I reminded him of Kismet once more. The engineer car and that of the Colonel began to move forward. Our car drove slowly behind.

We continued to crawl at a snail's pace along the broken highway. Telegraph poles leaned at strange angles; burned tanks and trucks lay on their backs like dead beetles. Every few moments we stopped while the engineer car ahead cautiously examined some particular spot in the road where a mine might be buried. Exactly how they located these mines I am still not fully aware, though I had a considerable education.

At two o'clock the convoy halted once more. I thought it was probably to eat lunch, for though four hours had elapsed we had traveled only twelve or fifteen miles.

The colonel came striding over from his car. "Sorry," he said. "Just had an order over the radio. This is as far as we go."

I was badly disappointed, for I had been looking forward more and more to this Beirut occupation. If I delayed much longer, it would be too late.

I asked the colonel if he objected to our traveling on alone.

His British brows tightened a little. "It's taking a bit of a chance. But I think we're over the worst. Go ahead if you like. Good luck."

We started up the road. We had gone on a little way when a group of bright-clad Syrian peasants appeared in the distance, working in a field at the side of the highway. The car came nearer and they caught sight of my British uniform as I sat with Alice beside the chauffeur. They took to their heels in terror, and disappeared into some fruit trees on a nearby hill.

I wondered for an instant at their panic. And then I remembered the reason. I had heard from our intelligence how enemy propaganda had told these Syrians over and over that the British and the Free French were lust-crazed monsters, who when they appeared would kill all the men and rape all the women. Ours was the first Allied car which had come down this highway since the Syrian war began. I was the terrible British Army. Alice, who had scorned a uniform and insisted on a fluffy dress bought in Hollywood, was that Army's monstrous woman.

A new group of peasants showed ahead at the edge of a village looking like the colored pictures at the back of a Bible, and another and another. They all darted off like sheep fleeing from an approaching tornado. Occasionally some braver soul would stand and wave timidly. I, feeling the entire weight of the British Army and the Empire on my shoulders, decided that such a response should not go unrewarded. I would bow graciously in answer, like a king on a triumphal tour.

The Lebanon Mountains rose starkly before us, a rocky

barrier two miles high that separated the desert from the Mediterranean. The road began to curve dizzily, with great gorges yawning far below where lonely eagles were flying. The Mad Demon, who had been driving soberly since our joining the convoy, began racing wildly again, whirling around the curves with screaming brakes, as though all the evil jinns of Arabia were speeding behind, seeking to snatch him off to hell.

We neared the top of the range and I saw a lonely post where two Vichy sentries stood outside a gateway, holding rifles. Other Vichy soldiers waited within, watching our approach in somber silence. We grew tense, not knowing what might happen. The car drew nearer. The two guards saw the uniform, seemed to hesitate an instant, then suddenly stiffened to attention and presented arms. The others inside the gate saluted rigidly. I saluted with a smile and bowed graciously again, the victor forgiving all.

We raced down the mountains in a new frenzy now, the shivering driver murmuring constantly to himself, as though he were repeating a charm. Farmhouses began to appear, and wide fields of waving grain, then Arabs driving burros and camels loaded with firewood. Off in the distance we saw Beirut, a flat sea of pastel-colored buildings, with pastel waves splashing up into the surrounding mountains. Beyond lay the Mediterranean, blue as the huge vats of dye in the street of the dyers at Damascus.

Suddenly the car stopped with a jolt that hurled us into the windshield again. The driver leaped outside and started racing frantically down the grassy slope. At first I thought he was deserting us, running for his life because of some deep mystery I could not fathom. Then I saw him rush up to a Syrian family, a blond fat man and woman and a quartet of blond children standing before a pink-roofed cottage, and embrace them fervently one by one.

He came back a moment later. "My cousins," he said with a beatific smile.

We reached the plain and soon were caught up in the usual feverish traffic of these Western outposts of the Orient: the sleek automobiles of rich Arab princes and the rickety carts of vegetable sellers, on the verge of collapse under their cargos of oranges or huge watermelons; the trucks loaded with barrels and packing cases and camels plodding under swaying bales of straw; the wildly-clanging trolleys and the donkeys standing immovable, utterly oblivious of the thwacking sticks of their profane masters.

We drove to a hotel and with the Mad Demon helped the paunchy Syrian owner carry in our weighty bags. Because of the cease-fire there had been rumors of a German air attack and all the bellboys had fled to the hills.

A Syrian in a gray burnoose strode up to me and spoke oilily. "You want nice suit of clothes, Sidi? You want pretty girl? Not living in a house. Living with her mother. You want nice box candied fruit, Sidi?"

I wish I could say we were the first to occupy the city, called by some the Paris of the Middle East. But the troops coming up from the battle zone in the south had preceded us and were already thronging the sidewalks, searching for cafés. However, we did occupy the eastern sector, and we did open up the road across the mountains, the famous road from Beirut to the city of the Street Called Straight.

For a week or two everything went peacefully. With the tension of the campaign ended, Beirut became a city on a holiday. The night club in our hotel was packed with Allied soldiers watching fat girls, lean girls, blonde girls, dark girls, girls from every country bordering the Mediterranean and far beyond, a bare-legged, sometimes bare-breasted United Nations, dancing and swaying in bored monotony.

The bellboys and the servants who had run off to the hills came back for a few days, then ran off again as some enemy planes flew over the city. When we came down to breakfast in the morning we could tell whether the war news was good or bad merely by looking at the number and the faces of the waiters in the dining room. The bellboys came back to stay at last, and we knew the danger for the moment was over.

The populace switched from favoring Vichy and the Germans to loving the Allies as easily as the red-fezzed taxi drivers shifted gears in their noisy automobiles. The luckless inhabitants here since long before the days of Christ had become accustomed to adapting themselves to new conquerors, as animals take on the protective coloration of their habitat and become green in a forest or in farming country become brown like the soil. I had bought the local newspaper on our arrival the day of the Occupation. Printed that morning while the Vichy troops were still in the city, it had fulsomely chanted the praises of the Germans. Now it was equally enthusiastic in lauding the Allies. The paper, like many American journals was in the habit of running a daily quotation under the masthead. I noticed one morning the selection was singularly appropriate. It was a quotation from some Latin classic: "All is variation and change."

More British and Australian and Free French soldiers arrived and then some pink-cheeked sailors off British warships, followed by more bare-legged girls. The gaiety of the city increased.

There was a blackout, but despite the occasional enemy planes overhead, no one paid much attention.

And then came the explosion.

12.
The Volcano Blows Up

There had been several hints of trouble before it happened. Until the Syrian armistice, with a few exceptions, the basic relations between the Free French and the British had been most harmonious, and frequently, as in Brazzaville, superlative. There was often a real affection, a genuine fraternity, completely denying the ancient tradition, as sacredly held as the Arabs about me held the Koran, that despite any Entente Cordiale the heads of their governments might create, Englishmen and Frenchmen must thoroughly dislike each other.

The armistice was as a poison ruining a victory banquet. The British military, however famous for their accomplishments on the field of battle, like all military men, have never been noted for the depth of their thinking or their subtlety. Attacked from almost every quarter of the compass, they were anxious to end the fighting in Syria and turn their guns in other directions. When the chance came for the cease-fire, they accepted it quickly. They were not too concerned about their Free French allies, who existed only with their help, and who were only a small, even though important part of the operation.

Bitterly, my Free French friends told me, by the terms of the Syrian armistice and the treaty to follow, it was the Vichyites who were treated by the British as equals and given every consideration; the Free French, if not ignored, were brusquely brushed aside as creatures much inferior to the Vichy French they had been fighting. They had given up their families and their country, they said, to risk their lives fighting beside the English. Now their reward was deep humiliation.

What the British military did not realize was the depth of the shock and shame these Free French soldiers had felt at their country's defeat and occupation by the Germans. It lay in their consciousness every moment, needing only a word, a gesture to set off a whole train of tragic remembrance. They were atoning for the sins of a whole nation, and were desperately in need of praise, of glory, that would give them a feeling of redemption. If the British military had been wise, instead of tending to merely accept the Free French contribution as natural, they would have exalted every slightest exploit to the skies.

With the Allied entry into Beirut and my story written, my journalistic duties were ended for the moment; I devoted myself again to my responsibilities as Ambassador. These were increasing rapidly as the arguments over the armistice and the treaty increased. Often I would meet my Free French friends in the hotel, and over a lunch or a drink, try to explain that their British opposite numbers were not treacherous, only stupid. Inflation was rampant in Beirut and the price of Scotch and martinis was high. More Paramount and dispatch money dissolved in this liquid diplomatic persuasion.

I met Cornelius Engert, the U.S. Consul at Beirut who

THE VOLCANO BLOWS UP

had negotiated the armistice, and was aiding in drawing up the terms of the treaty. I informed him of the unhappy state of mind of the Free French and suggested to him and my British friends it would be wise if similar humiliation was avoided in the future.

Beirut meanwhile was booming. The crowded streets were becoming bedlam; the money changers were thick as fleas in the bazaars. New generals and diplomats were pouring in by plane and car; the hotel night club, the thermometer that always indicated the Beirut temperature, was crowded almost to suffocation.

There came a breath like a cool wind sweeping the desert, as my beloved General Sicé, recently made High Commissioner of Free French Africa, suddenly flew in from Brazzaville to take part in the treaty negotiations. My unofficial ambassadorship from the Free French to the United States was now out of the pages of Alice In Wonderland; it was I who presented General Sicé to Consul Engert, the official American negotiator.

The General and I dined at Engert's house, and I again pointed out the increasing French bitterness, which General Sicé's arrival had further crystallized. Unless the British attitude were changed, grave trouble was certain.

I had several visits alone with Engert, quite pleasant visits always, though I felt my enthusiasm was a puzzle to him. A dry individual, reminding me of a high-school Latin teacher, he was trying scrupulously hard to be fair. He had few of those unreasoning pro-Vichy prejudices

205

which I found among some of our diplomats, over whom I shall charitably draw a veil.

It was a fitting time for an explosion, hot, stifling, with the soldiers and the diplomats going off, every moment they could snatch, to the nearby beaches or the picturesque hamlets high in the Lebanon Mountains. With my diplomatic activities steadily intensifying, I went to the mountains as well, crossing the towering ranges to Damascus, dodging in and out once more between the heavy-laden donkeys and camels, a spectacular journey that seemed pallid and dull without the Mad Demon. My trips soon made me almost a commuter between the two cities, as a denizen of Madison Avenue commutes between New York and Connecticut. On each of my trips to the Syrian metropolis I met the Princess Atrach again, still sweeping like a twentieth-century Scheherazade down the grand stairway of the hotel. Each time she again invited me to come for a visit to Es Soueida. Alice, who had now met her as well, flatteringly insisted that I possessed for the princess an irresistible attraction. But, alas, I was sure I was not the sort to sweep dazzling Oriental princesses off their jewel-slippered feet. The reason, I knew, was much less romantic. I was the author of a successful motion picture whose fame had reached even to Damascus. The princess had acted in the films, and like any actress was still film struck, even though she was now the Emira. This was not a case of my non-existent sex appeal; it was my some-what diluted film glamor.

I had long been wanting to see this once-forbidden Druse capital of which I had heard so much, and which rumor made seem as mysterious as the headquarters of the Grand Llama in Tibet. Now that Alice was with me I felt there would be no danger of misunderstanding. I accepted the invitation and waited with eagerness for the appointed weekend to arrive.

The Princess called for us in a magnificent car, and we set off toward the Druse Mountains. She sat in front, her almond-shaped eyes emitting green, electric flashes as she turned now and then to talk to the two handsome, richly-turbaned princes, her cousins, sitting at her side.

Sitting with us was another passenger of whom, like the Princess, I had often heard before our meeting, an individual who with his blond hair and trim moustache and trim, erect figure might have played the part in an English film of a youngish general reviewing the cadets at Sandhurst Academy, so completely was he the picture of a perfect British officer. It was Air Commodore Buss, holder of one of the highest posts in the Intelligence Service, and reputed to know more about the Arabs than any other Englishman alive.

Whenever an Arab crisis occurred, and they occurred with the same certainty that the sun rose over the Leb-anon, it was Air Commodore Buss who the grave Eng-lishmen sitting about a conference table in the Foreign

Office first called on for his opinions; it was on his advice they so often acted in making their decisions. A veteran of the deserts since the first World War, it was Air Commodore Buss, who to succeed Lawrence of Arabia, had picked the now legendary Glubb Pacha and brought him to Transjordan where he had organized the Arabs into a fierce fighting Legion.

It was Buss, I knew, who single-handed had persuaded the Princess Atrach to bring her husband and the Druse to the side of the Allies. Because of his own nature and that of his work he would have no publicity, letting the fruits of his labors and the honors go to others. He was one of those unsung heroes, known only to the few at the summit, to whom England owes its greatness.

As he sat on the other side of Alice in the back seat of the car, with caravans of camels rolling past and women carrying jars of water on their heads as Ruth carried water in the days of the Bible, there occurred again one of those strange happenings, one of those fantastic accidents of fate which make all our careful planning seem so foolish. I have a faculty, perhaps after many years of studying this queer human race, of knowing the people who are going to be my friends on sight. Buss and I exchanged a few words, and formed an instant friendship. It was a friendship that within twenty-four hours had spectacular consequences. If we hadn't become such friends he wouldn't have invited me to the reception the next morning. And if I hadn't gone to the reception. . . .

As we rode along I heard from him some of the stories about the Druse and the strange rituals of their religion known to none except the Druse even to this day. I learned the answer to a riddle which had somewhat puzzled me; why the Druse were generally considered favorable to the British. From Buss I heard how many years before a Druse leader, fleeing from his enemies, was given shelter by an Englishman. The Druse had never forgotten, and were devoted to the British ever since.

The passing camels ceased now. The highway became deserted, empty. Mile after mile we drove, choking with dust, as the car sped on faster. We were in territory once part of the old Roman Empire. Bleak ruins of ancient Roman villages appeared, sometimes with the toppled pillars and arches of what might have been a temple. Even the road was the old Roman road the Legions of the Caesars had traveled, with here and there some flagstones still showing the ruts worn by the wheels of the Roman chariots.

A caravan appeared moving in the direction of Baghdad, then some herders driving a flock of dusty sheep. Near them was a lonely Druse riding a mottled horse, perhaps come over from some solitary desert castle to inspect his baaing property. He bowed deeply to the Emira and the princes in the car.

The highway grew empty once more. The road narrowed and began to cross an endless desert of black lava, with gloomy lava rocks on either side standing like rows of enormous coffins, as though set out for dead giants who had been the inhabitants. Black dust flew up in clouds. Our faces and hands darkened as if we had been shoveling coal.

The sun began to set over the funereal landscape. Some black huts appeared made of the same lava as the countryside, then more flocks of baaing sheep and maaing goats on the way to their pens and stables for the night. The huts grew closer together, and formed a black, melancholy street. We were in Es Soueida, the Druse capital.

We drove on to what I expected to be the palace of the Emira. We stopped after a few moments before the royal residence, and I stared in amazement. It was a perfect Hollywood bungalow. We went inside, and I became even more incredulous. It was an exact copy of those buildings which exist by the hundreds and the thousands in the shadow of the Hollywood hills and beside the white sands of Malibu, complete with Hollywood bar. The princess had carried her film ideas very far.

I tried to imagine where she could have found the materials for the house, and how after they were located had brought them to this remote spot in the Syrian desert; whether they had come by truck or camel-back or infinite journeys of infinite donkeys. I gave up trying to answer my own questions.

The Emir came forward, a handsome figure, who made us welcome with the smiling hospitality for which the

Druse are famous. Soon guests began arriving for dinner to meet us; Brigadier Bell, the bright young general in charge of the British troops in the area; the Free French commandant and his aide, with whom I exchanged some news of mutual friends; and perhaps a score of Druse chieftains from the nearby countryside, magnificent figures with long beards and flowing robes, who looked as if they might be old Hebrew patriarchs assembled to draw up some new commandments for the Bible.

But there was no solemnity such as I imagined with patriarchs. Either these were different than the Biblical variety or patriarchs were different than I thought. As we sat down at a long table in the Hollywood dining room, there was only jollity and merriment. Most of them spoke no English or French, and I knew in those days perhaps two or three hundred words of Arabic. But this seemed not the slightest barrier.

With the help of the princess and Air Commodore Buss, who spoke Arab dialects like a native, we held a never-ceasing, gay conversation. They would tell me Arab jokes about wily Arabs whose wiles didn't succeed and I countered with American stories about the dumb hillbilly who had never seen ice and the dog that played chess with his master. My jokes were received with such enthusiasm I began to run out of material, and thought up all the supposedly funny stories I could remember from my childhood. They roared with laughter and demanded more. Rarely had I encountered such an appreciative audience.

The dinner was a gourmet's delight, such as I had never enjoyed in the Middle East, innumerable courses of exotic meats and strange vegetables, topped off by a dozen varieties of pahklava and sweets, and several kinds of coffee.

The party ended after midnight, a glorious success by any standard.

We bade the Emir and the Emira goodnight, and Buss came to our room for a chat.

For perhaps an hour we talked about the fantastic Middle East, and I listened fascinated to the tales of his early days among the Arabs. I was sorry when he looked at his watch and saw that it was time to go to bed.

In the morning we took an early breakfast together.

"The tribes are having a little reception for me in a couple of hours," he said across a steaming cup of tea. "It's to celebrate our victory over the Vichyites. Perhaps you and your wife would like to come along."

We went soon after to a drab stone building that served as the equivalent of the Es Soueida City Hall, and entered a barren room where perhaps a hundred richly-turbaned Druse chiefs were gathered, among them most of the long-bearded patriarchs with whom I had talked so merrily the night before. One after another they moved to where Buss was standing with us, and facing him, made the usual polite Arabic speeches, full of poetry and flowery references to the classics, and quotations from the Koran. Suddenly, even with my almost complete ignorance of the language, I noticed a distinct change in the tenor of what they were saving. Their pleasant words became a harsh staccato; their smiling faces grew grim. I whispered to Buss and asked what was happening.

"I don't know," he answered. His blue eyes mirrored his anxiety. "Something's up. I can't tell what so far. Whatever it is, it's not pleasant."

A new chief took the floor and another. The speeches grew angrier, and now were punctuated with fiery gestures.

"They're beginning to attack the French," whispered Buss. "They say they can't tell any difference between the Free French and the Vichy French. They say all Frenchmen are alike."

I knew the reason that prompted their denunciation. For many years they had been exploited by a short-sighted French colonialism until in 1926 their wrath had broken forth in the fierce revolt that had occasioned so many French military funerals. Their active resistance had been crushed at last, but not their spirit. Their bitterness against the French had been only intensified, like the gathering steam in a long-pent-up volcano, waiting for a chance to explode.

The talks became orations, always longer, always wilder. The faces of the men with whom I had joked so

213

lightly the night before were now tense with wrath and hatred. They seemed like the fabled lion with a sting in his tail, lashing themselves into fury.

The crowd moved off to the nearby home of one of the bearded Druse leaders, more like the imaginary palace I had conceived as the residence of the Emira. We entered a lofty-arched hall and sat down at an immense table loaded with coffee and pahklava and bowls of pomegranates and bananas. The chiefs filed in behind us and took their places in silence.

For a moment they sat there motionless, and I thought perhaps they were praying. Then a flashing-eyed, black-bearded figure clad in shining silk arose, and the denunciations began again, one moment icy with bitterness, the next flaming with passion.

One of the long-robed patriarchs who had sat near me at the dinner stood up now and spoke, his voice trembling with emotion. "Vichy French, Free French. We hate all the French. All rotten. We want the French to leave the Druse country. We want the French to get out of Syria."

Buss arose now and in his soothing voice that had calmed many an Arab storm, attempted to reason with them and assuage their wrath. His words were useless as a man with a garden hose trying to put out a raging oil fire in Oklahoma. Another speaker stood up, calling on Allah to punish the French wickedness.

Alice and I sat as in a spell, hypnotized by the scene being enacted before us. A Druse leader whom I had not seen before, a tall, smooth-shaven figure wearing a magnificent burnoose trimmed with green and gold, arose and began a new long oration. I listened intently, trying to understand, for like some of the others he occasionally lapsed into French.

It is curious how in times of great crisis we think of insignificant, almost ridiculous details. There is no slightest reason why, but I remember almost more vividly than anything else that fantastic day a bowl of fruit standing on the table directly before me. It contained two pomegranates, a huge Damascus orange and a ripe banana.

I had taken the banana absently, and was removing the peel, when the man in the magnificent burnoose suddenly broke off his impassioned speech and turned toward me, his face rigid beneath his sumptuous turban, his words cold, stinging, like pellets of ice.

"You are an American writer," he said in French. "We want you to tell the world that Vichy French, Free French, we see no difference. We loathe and despise all the French. We want you to tell the world that unless the French leave Syria, we, the Druse, will quit the war."

I can still rarely eat a banana without thinking of that moment at the table in the lofty-arched hall of the bearded chief in the far-off, gloomy Druse mountains. For the implications of his words were so catastrophic as to stagger the imagination. The Druse, who had played such a vital part in gaining the victory in Syria, were the keystone of this entire section of the Allied line. If they

215

quit the war, with this encouragement, the German in-spired rebels in Iraq would be apt to rise again. All the bitter fighting just ended might well be wasted and a whole new series of disasters begun.

I mumbled some kind of lame, non-committal answer. A novelist, accustomed to writing at my leisure, I do not have apt lines ready for any emergency. I reserve these only for my heroes.

The group at the table broke up soon after. Buss and I walked slowly outside with Alice, too shocked for a moment to speak. We left Alice at the home of the Emira and Buss and I hurried over to the office of Brigadier Bell, the British Commander, to tell him of the catastrophe.

It would now have been apparent to a blind man what was going to happen. For many years the British and the French, the two great colonial powers, had been battling for control of the Middle East landbridge, with the British usually winning. The Free French were already smarting under the humiliation of the recent armistice; they would be certain this was a new trick of British imperialism to throw them out of Syria, the one area they possessed.

Until late afternoon, Buss and Bell and I sat discussing what could be done, then had a little food and resumed our conference. Hour after hour we talked, until far into the night, trying to foresee every possible contin-gency. By three o'clock in the morning we had decided on a definite course of action. Brigadier Bell would try

216

to pacify the Druse in Soueida and attempt to persuade them to soften their position. Buss and I would cut the weekend short and return at once to Beirut. Buss would report to General Wilson, known as Jumbo, the commander of the Allied Armies. I would call on Consul Engert, the American negotiator of the armistice and explain what had happened. After that I would see my Free French friends, and assuring them this was not the usual trick they expected of perfidious England, urge them not to get excited.

I was an Ambassador now with a vengeance.

I was faced with another decision as well. In my newspaper days I had always prided myself on being a good reporter. This was an event of world importance. As a correspondent it was another world scoop, which I could manage to smuggle past the censorship in some neutral diplomatic pouch or by some returning traveler. But it was news which if sent would have tragic consequences. I chose the moral right as against journalism, and wrote nothing.

We drove to Beirut in the morning, and as we expected, found that the news had spread far and wide, and the Free French were already raging. Buss took me to meet General Wilson, a huge, jovial man, who in appearance reminded me of a great, genial cinnamon bear of the sort that asks the passing automobilist for food in a national park out West. I then took Buss to call on Engert. Despite the appalling situation I could not help smiling when Engert turned to Buss, and indicating me, remarked, "representing Free France," and the quick-witted Buss, correcting him, added, "and Free America." Idealist and innocent that I was, the significance of Engert's words did not dawn upon me until several years later. Idealists are rare in diplomacy, especially in the Middle East. I am sure the good Mr. Engert believed me firmly in the Free French pay.

I explained to Engert, on the basis of my intimate relationship with the Free French, what I felt was certain to happen, then went on to see my French friends to explain that this crisis was the creation of the Druse, not a Machiavellian scheme hatched at 10 Downing Street, a sinister British intrigue. For days we talked and my drink bills soared and my Paramount funds shrank further. But the effort and the money was not wasted. The French knew my complete objectivity and knew there was no reason for my not telling the truth; the situation grew more hopeful.

And then General De Gaulle arrived from London, a vial of wrath, who would listen to no one but himself, and all my work and my drinks were undone. Months later, during the extraordinary sequence of events which followed, I wrote to Lord Halifax after I met with him in Washington:

". . . . With all the respect that I have for General De Gaulle, with all my appreciation of his accomplishments and sacrifices . . . . (he) seems to be a natural trouble maker. I am convinced that the Syrian problem would have been settled with comparative ease had he not been present. He was always inflaming the reasonable men to anger. I know this to my sorrow; as I told you, hour after hour I labored in Beirut and the suburbs of Lebanon, trying to pour oil on troubled waters, only to find De Gaulle creating new storms, new crises. . . ."

I saw General Speers who on previous occasions had always been so cordial, and tried to tell him what had really happened. A blind worshiper of De Gaulle, he became very angry, and would not listen. I heard that a little later he became De Gaulle's bitterest enemy.

De Gaulle's aides suggested that I see him again and write another interview for America. I was much too angry and ignored the invitation.

With the passing days De Gaulle's wrath intensified. As I wrote further to Lord Halifax:

". . . . He (De Gaulle) strikes me as a man of keen talents, but of the ascetic, schoolmaster type, with a decided tendency toward mental arrogance, and an unwillingness to listen to the other person's point of view. I think he would be very difficult at a peace conference. . . . Whenever he meets other men, he makes enemies. . . . Unless there has been a revolutionary change in his character, his usefulness in those areas (the Middle East and Africa) is unquestionably and irrevocably at an end. . . ."

The crisis grew, and Free French-British relations which had been so amicable, deteriorated with the speed of the poison of a viper, striking from behind a rock in the desert. All the centuries-old lies were retold, the ancient suspicions and enmities revived. The deterioration affected the leaders as well. I did not realize that morning as I sat at the table peeling the banana, how I was watching the beginning of the famous Churchill-De Gaulle quarrel.

I saw the princess, whose home we had left so unceremoniously, a number of times later in Damascus, always regally beautiful, always more and more mysterious. I was riding one day in the back seat of her car with a young British intelligence officer and I made a remark which took for granted that she was aiding the Allies as before. The officer, pretending to roll a cigarette, wrote something on a cigarette paper and flashed it before me. I read the pencilled words swiftly: "Better not talk. We don't know which side she's on now."

An instant later he lit a match and burned the paper to ashes.

I was in New York after the war when I happened to pick up a newspaper and saw with a shock that she was dead, killed the night before in an automobile accident on the Riviera. I heard queer stories later that it was no accident. Rumor said it was a typical mid-Eastern plot, arranged by some ruthless political enemies.

Poor beautiful Princess Atrach. She left life as she lived it, in a mystery melodrama where she always played the lead.

220

The war news became blacker again. The Germans were sweeping across the Russian steppes; the relief the Allies had counted upon as the result of the Soviet invasion had failed to materialize. The blitz in England was killing new helpless civilians every night; the submarines were sinking ever more and more ships. It appeared as if the Germans would carry out Hitler's boast. They were the Master Race.

The rift between the French and the British continued to deepen. Some of my Free French friends, influenced by the success of my reports to America, suggested that I go on to London. They suggested that in the British capital I present their case to Churchill and his advisers; and explaining the situation to the other French leaders there besides De Gaulle, try to restore relations to their earlier happier state.

I was not willing to carry my ambassadorial duties that far. After all I was a journalist, with certain responsibilities. So I did not agree.

I did not know that I would shortly change my mind.

13.
The Father With the Little Chin

The Middle East—Arabia, Transjordan, Iran and the rest—even in peace time had been like super-dry tinder, ready to burst into flame at a spark from a soldier's cigarette. Now in wartime, with the Druse crisis and the rebels in Iraq and the threat of a German parachute invasion, new disaster seemed certain every instant, as when a truck loaded with nitro-glycerine, races without brakes down a hill.

The situation was made worse by the fact that General Wavell, commander of the North African and Middle East forces, had just been relieved of his command, with all the consequent disorganization that always follows. Almost simultaneously came the news that the Australians, worried about the fate of their superb troops at Tobruk, had brought about the downfall of their own Dominion government. Moreover, Iran with the Russians on one side and the British on the other, was in a feverish ferment. It was little wonder that there came rumors of new German-inspired revolts and conspiracies everywhere.

I had been hearing more and more frequently now of Buss's friend, Glubb Pasha, who had just played such a vital role in defeating the rebels in Iraq. Like Leclerc, he would strike in the manner of a crafty desert animal, always when he was least expected, appearing from nowhere with his armored cars and his camels, and then disappearing like a jinn risen from a bottle into the sandy wastes from which he had come. So sudden and devastating were his attacks, so fearful the damage he wrought that the Germans, seeking to lessen the terror associated with his name, announced that he had died in action. But he was still very much alive, waiting in the desert again, ready to pounce upon any luckless invader.

It became necessary for Air Commodore Buss to visit this spectacular soldier, known to his men as the Father With The Little Chin.

He invited Alice and myself to come along. We crossed the border into Palestine next day, with huge tanks and Bren carriers rumbling on the roads once more like ugly, prehistoric animals. High above us German planes droned and whined, taking reconnaisance photos, until a British fighter would soar up, and with a noisy chattering of its machine guns drive them away. Once in the shade of a halted tank, we saw a young shepherd piping to his flock grazing peacefully nearby, as the boy Joseph might have piped to his flock thousands of years before.

We stopped for the night in Jerusalem at the King David Hotel where I had left Alice some weeks before, the modern substitute in the Holy City for King Solomon's Palace. Through its high-vaulted doorways passed the war-time substitutes for kings, the flawlessly dressed diplomats and gold-starred generals.

We made a quick visit to the old town, appearing little changed since the time of Christ, except that instead of Roman soldiers carrying spears in the streets there were now British soldiers carrying rifles. We entered the Holy Sepulcher, watched over by a drowsy Arab, placed there, said the legend, because the various groups of Christians could not agree on which sect should guard the tomb, and so were compelled to choose a non-believer, a living symbol of the difficulties humanity faced before it could attain universal brotherhood.

We set off in the morning for Transjordan, and soon were in a desert of rocks and clay and sand bleak as the Sahara. The Dead Sea showed in the distance. But instead of the tinkling caravans of the Bible there were now huge trucks filled with phosphates and chemicals to make ammunition.

A Bedouin encampment of forty or fifty tents showed ahead, with a vast herd of fat camels. As we drew near a dozen warlike Arabs carrying long rifles passed, riding sleek white horses.

Buss watched the newcomers move slowly off into the desert. "Before Glubb came those chaps on the horses would have been raiders," he remarked. "They'd have swept down on that camp like a sandstorm." He offered me a cigarette from a thin silver case. "It was a regular sport, this raiding, with elaborate rules, like cricket. Livestock was the best thing to steal, preferably camels. Only a crude player took money or property, and capturing a woman was the worst kind of luck. The code demanded that she be given a camel and sent back home."

We passed some villages of Circassians, tall men like

those I had seen in Syria, despite the heat still wearing the same tall fur hats as their ancestors in their far off mountain homeland, testimony to the tenacity of the habits which rule humankind.

Amman came into view, the ancient Philadelphia, the City of Brotherly Love, once a great capital of the Romans. The old Roman theater, almost perfectly preserved, could still seat 40,000 people. Now the settlement was a collection of dull yellowish buildings, climbing a little way up the sides of naked yellow mountains.

We learned that Glubb Pasha was holding a review of his troops for the Emir of Transjordan at a nearby camp. We hurried out, and arriving during an intermission in the ceremonies, met him and Abdullah, the Emir. The review over, we sauntered off with Glubb to where a canopy of gaudy-dyed camels' wool was stretched on poles as protection from the desert sun, which seemed almost as powerful as that of the Tchad. I sat down next him on a scarlet-embroidered cushion. A small man with a pink and white complexion and bright eyes peering out with a touch of humor from beneath his colored turban, I saw at once the reason for his nickname, the Father With The Little Chin. The lower part of his jaw and his chin had been shattered, obviously by an enemy bullet.

We sat chatting and drinking coffee, while the soldiers of the Arab Legion stole like ghosts in and out the tent. If the costumes at Mao in the Sahara would have served for scenes in a desert opera, the costumes here would have been perfect for some wildly imagined spectacle in the Russian Ballet. Each Arab was clad in a gorgeous flowing robe and his head was crowned with a brilliant colored turban; from under the turban, his black hair, uncut perhaps since birth, trailed in long shiny tresses down his back, sometimes almost to the waist. Long bandoliers of cartridges were crossed over each man's shoulders. In each broad belt at intimidating intervals was a wicked-looking dagger. Ironically these fantastic warriors who were the terror of the desert bore a very unterrifying nickname; because of their long hair, demanded by tribal custom, they were known to every British Tommy and Australian as Glubb's Girls.

It was no surprise to learn that these costumes had been designed by Glubb Pacha himself. From his speech, it was obvious that even though a soldier he was an artist as well. It was curious how in the desert one found these men, Englishmen and Frenchmen alike, Buss himself, Glubb Pacha, Leclerc, the French officers at Mao and the merry commandant of the Camel Troops beyond, all with a profound sense of beauty. The desert, which had given men most of their great religions, inspired them in other ways as well.

This Arab Legion was perhaps the easiest-going, least-disciplined army in the world, the sort of army a weary private dreams about as he lies exhausted at night on his cot, after being screamed at all day by hard-bitten sergeants and corporals. For discipline is the one thing the Bedouin, free as the eagle drifting over the dunes, would die rather than accept. There were bugle calls at intervals but if a soldier chanced not to respond, there was no hoarse command, "Sergeant, take that man's name." Before a battle Glubb Pasha assembled his troops, and told them the complete plan of action. If the men approved, they told him so with enthusiasm; if they failed to agree and had a better suggestion, Glubb Pasha adopted the amendment. It was a complete denial of the old Prussian system, that a soldier must be an automaton, giving instant and unquestioning obedience. Here every soldier in the Legion was a king.

We drove over to the white-walled house soon after where Glubb lived with his pretty English wife, presiding over the household in this strange land as calmly as though she had just stepped in from a lovely English garden. In his study, decorated with jeweled scimitars and other gifts of sheiks and native princes, I saw a map of the desert, with black dots here and there in the midst of the empty desolation.

"Water holes," explained Glubb Pasha. "Wherever there's water we build a fort. Everybody has to drink sometime. The man who controls the water controls the desert."

We set out in the morning to see the dots become reality, Alice and myself, an Arab driver, and Glubb's second in command, Major Lash, a tall, bronzed Englishman wearing an Arab headdress, almost as picturesque a figure as Glubb himself. The yellow hills of Amman soon became a trackless waste of dunes, so white and dazzling in the sunlight, that when I took off my dark glasses for a moment to wipe the sweat and drifting sand from my face my eyes burned painfully.

The heat increased as the day advanced. Beautiful blue lakes appeared in the distance, with rows of buildings lining the shore, and groves of lofty palms. I knew there was no water or no city within many miles, and that, as in the Sahara, I was only seeing a mirage.

Camel bones lay here and there, and now and then a mound of smaller bones of some other animal, perhaps a man, who had wandered from his caravan and died of thirst. Occasionally a vulture, high overhead, would swoop down and flapping its wings gloomily, fly low over the car as though making a grim survey for a future meal. Off in the distance a solitary gazelle bounded along the top of a dune, like the imprisoned spirit of some enchanted prince in an Arab fairy tale.

Up and down the dunes we coursed, while the driver, silent as though he were a deafmute, kept his eyes fixed steadily on the sand, like the driver in the Tchad watching every slightest change of color and texture.

Unlike the Sahara, he drove without a compass. I marveled how he could go so surely over these ever-shifting waves of sand without even a single tire track as a guide.

229

I mentioned this to the turbaned Major.

"Their sense of direction is uncanny," he replied. "I'll let you see for yourself."

We reached an area where the dunes gave way to a gravelly clay, and there was no danger of sinking in the sand. The Major halted the driver sharply.

"Ask him to show you Baghdad," he said to me quietly.

I did as he suggested.

Without an instant's hesitation the driver raised his hand and pointed off to the east.

The Major compared the direction with a compass and a map. The Arab's pointing finger was exact.

"And now Es Sait. . . . Now Ezrak."

Each time it was as though the pointing finger was the needle of the compass.

A stone tower appeared on the horizon, as we approached becoming a tiny fortress surrounded by a maze of barbed wire. It was one of the dots on the map, built around a well.

Two sentries stood before the narrow gateway and saluted smartly. We went inside and found it a Mao in miniature, with a few camels groomed like velvet groaning dismally and some amiable Glubb's Girls practicing with a machine gun. I could not help wondering what happened in the heat of a battle when the feeder of the machine gun became tangled in one of those long tresses of hair. We drank Turkish coffee with the Arab officer in charge, and continued over the dunes.

The mountains of sand suddenly gave way to a great mud flat, the dry bed of an ancient lake, now covered with a shiny black clay so that it appeared like a gigantic unfinished bowl, ready for the potter's furnace. I learned that Lawrence of Arabia had used this smooth expanse as a race track for his men who drove armored cars when he wished to give them some excitement on a holiday. We too, raced across it, wishing the whole desert had such a perfect surface. The mud flat in turn gave way to an ancient lava flow, like that of the Druse country, black, funereal. Beyond, at the top of a long rise, appeared a castle, dazzling white, like a magic palace out of the fairy tale of the enchanted gazelle. I thought at first it was another mirage. It proved to be real, the ruins of an ancient palace built by some sultan or emperor to control the caravan routes and levy a tax on every traveler who chanced to pass that way, or hold the wealthier merchants for ransom.

We went through the doorway. Huge lizards crawled sluggishly over the ornate mosaic floors where once the mighty prince or Khan had walked in splendor; in the rooms that had been the quarters of his wives, huge wasps had built their nests and buzzed about us in noisy menace.

All day we drove, occasionally passing a caravan or more Bedouin encampments, with the black tents silhouetted behind the grazing camels. Near one of the tents a stern, regally-clad Arab was just setting out for the hunt, holding on his wrist a chained falcon, with eyes as fierce as those of its haughty master.

Darkness fell, but it brought no halt in our sandy pilgrimage, and only a slight cooling of the fiery air. Then a tiny black lake appeared, reflecting the twinkling stars overhead in tiny points of light like matches thrown on pitch. Some shadowy tents showed along the shore, where hooded Arabs sat, vaguely illumined by sputtering torches or acetylene lamps, then another stone tower, dimly outlined against the stars. It was Ezrak, one of the principal bases of Glubb's Legion. We washed with water an Arab poured from a jar, and went off to a tent where a score of Arab soldiers were waiting, sitting crosslegged around a hissing lamp.

A feast had been prepared in our honor, like that at Mao, a whole roast sheep resting on an enormous tray. We ate, being careful to use only our right hands; we had been warned by Glubb Pasha that using the left was an unpardonable insult.

An Arab soldier brought out a lute, and began to sing in the strange Arab falsetto that sounds as if the singer were holding his nose with his fingers, and which legend says arose in trying to imitate the flute. He was followed by an Arab chanting a long monotonous poem, accompanied by the staccato beating of a drum. I learned that after a Legion battle, when the dead were buried and the wounded cared for, there was always such a ballad, composed by some poetically inclined soldier, reciting all that had happened, and telling both the blame and the glory.

Two days later we were back in Jerusalem with Air Commodore Buss and the sleek diplomats and the generals in the grandeur of the King David Hotel.

For some time I had been anxious to return to Cairo, which with the replacement of Wavell and the growing strength of Rommel, had become once more the center of intense political and military activity.

An RAF land convoy was leaving for Cairo next morning. We joined it and that night were installed again in the Continental Hotel, swarming with British officers in their colorful uniforms of the Cherry Pickers and the Coldstream Guards and the languorous, perfumed spies.

The tensity in the city had increased markedly since our earlier visit. Egyptian officials, confident the Germans would soon take over the country, were growing increasingly hostile to anyone like myself in Allied uniform. The Germans themselves were increasing their pressure. Air raid alarms were constant now. The intervals between the last all clear and the new alert grew shorter and shorter. But it seemed to be merely a tactic of terror, for the planes droning overhead like sleepy mosquitoes each time failed to drop any bombs. We decided to go to a picture show, and came out of the theater after seeing the film Waterloo Bridge, part of which took place in a German air attack. We found our-

233

selves in the Cairo street with the searchlights sweeping through the sky everywhere above us and the sirens wailing dolefully in warning. It was difficult to separate the imagined raid we had just witnessed from the reality.

We had been in the hotel perhaps three nights when the Germans struck at last. We were awakened about two o'clock in the morning by a terrific explosion. Looking out I saw a building not too far from the hotel burst into flames and heard the telltale drone of aircraft. An instant later the tragic symphony that was an air raid had begun, a symphony of sound and sight composed by a musician using noises instead of notes and an artist employing lights instead of tubes of color. First there flashed the white beams of the searchlights, piercing the blackness in vivid flickering patterns like an extraordinary Aurora Borealis. After these appeared the tracer bullets, leaving fantastic green and golden trails as though they were curious snails writing in the black void of space. Now and then a giant flare floated down, dropped by the enemy so that he could better see to find his prey, and the delicate Very lights, beautiful beads of color loosed by the English fighters in signal so they would not be fired upon by their own men. Occasionally there was a new blinding glow as a new doomed building leaped into flames.

All the while as accompaniment there came the chatter of machine guns and the thunder of anti-aircraft and the screaming sirens of military vehicles racing through the streets, then the final crescendo, the rumble like an earthquake of an exploding bomb.

I took Alice downstairs where she would be safer in case the hotel was hit. The lobby was a panorama of the war in the Middle East, roused suddenly from its sleep. Drowsy-eyed generals clad in pajamas and dressing gowns sat in chairs or on lounges, looking bored or slightly annoyed as though interrupted when they held a good hand at bridge. The spies, beautiful in night-gowns slightly concealed by luxurious silk robes sat stiffly, perhaps resentful that they had not been spared this indignity by their employers. Here and there were young government employees, accompanied by pretty girls they had been squiring at a dance in the hotel, talking and laughing above the roar of the guns. The poor native waiters, unused to war, were a sickly gray with terror; when they brought a drink, their hands were shaking.

The all-clear sounded. The fiery painting in the sky, visible through the doorway and the windows, slowly faded into nothingness. The symphony ended.

The disastrous defeats suffered by the Russians should have brought the Free French and the British together again, as a common danger unites even the fiercest enemies. But instead the breach only became wider. The Churchill-De Gaulle quarrel continued to grow in bitterness.

My Free French friends urged me once more to jour-

235

ney on to London. They pointed out that only three non-Druse individuals had been a witness to the episode at Es Soueida, which had shattered Franco-British amity, Air Commodore Buss and Alice and myself. Buss, a loyal English officer, was obviously ruled out as prejudiced; that left only ourselves as objective observers. My French friends argued that both they and the British knew my only motive was to help defeat the Germans and win the war. Moreover, they declared, due to the extraordinary circumstances which had taken me to the Congo and Ubangui-Shari and the Tchad, as well as Syria and Egypt, I had been in a position to observe the workings of the Free French-British alliance as no other person. If I went to England and saw Churchill and the British and Free French leaders, and told them exactly what had happened at Es Soueida, as well as my ideas about what should be done to restore the former unity, perhaps my efforts as a peacemaker would bear fruit, as they had borne fruit for a brief time in Beirut.

I suppose, looking back over all the fantastic things which occurred, the suggestion was eminently logical. But I was still reluctant about its adoption. Egypt was becoming more and more journalistically exciting. With the ever-increasing difficulties of transportation, I was sure that if I ever left, I would probably never return. I discussed the matter with my English friends, and they felt as the French. It was well worth the trial.

I think I might have still refused except that subconsciously I felt a physical slowing down which I would not admit, a foretaste of the effects of the fever-laden mosquitoes which Africa in those days gave as permanent souvenirs to so many of her visitors.

I agreed to go.

A few days later we climbed aboard another huge Sunderland flying boat bound on the long, roundabout trip for England. In my pocket were letters to members of the Morton Committee who were to take me direct to Churchill.

The plane took off, and the Pyramids and the tawny Sphinx vanished in the desert. Now eager with anticipation, I studied a map of our route, dropping south to below the Equator, westward to Lagos, and then on to bomb-torn London.

We never did arrive.

14.
The Americans Who Stayed to Dinner

The trip south, which took four or five days, was a succession of deserts gradually changing to jungles and Negro boys at three in the morning shaking us in a hotel bed and murmuring apologetically, "Time to get up, Master. Time to get up, Madam," as they thrust a cup of bitter black tea into our mouths.

The early hour was made necessary because the planes did not fly at night through fear of accident. The river or lake airports were sometimes almost two hours' drive away, and the pilots wished to take advantage of every moment of daylight.

Cairo became Wadi Halfa, Wadi Halfa merged into Khartoum, Khartoum changed to Kampala in Uganda, Kampala became Stanleyville and Elizabethville in the Belgian Congo. Hour after hour we flew over the equatorial forest, in the morning mist spread out below us like an endless dirty green blanket, touched here and there with splotches of mold. Even at the height we were flying we could detect the curious mixture of odors that I had learned to know so well, the smell of rotting giant trees and plants that never saw the sun, of ant hills and elephants and crocodiles in stagnant pools, the smell of the jungle.

It seemed insane to be coming this enormous distance south when actually we wished to go north to England. But the German control of the Western Mediterranean and North Africa made it necessary. By following the

Nile and continuing on south of the Sahara, the huge flying boats could find rivers and lakes all the way to the Congo and across the continent to West Africa.

Like the Clipper crossing the Atlantic, the passengers were military and diplomatic. I talked most often with Arthur Dawe, Assistant Undersecretary of State for the Colonial Office, Rear Admiral King, one of the heroes of the invasion of Crete, and the wife of Free French General Le Gentilhomme on her way to join her husband in Brazzaville.

We arrived at Leopoldville, and I hurried across the river to visit General Sicé, now installed at Brazzaville in the office of the High Commissioner. There I met his youthful and buoyant aide, Richard Roussy de Sales, newly arrived from New York, who brought me the news that compensated for many bleak hours; my dispatches as a journalist had succeeded where my efforts as an ambassador had dismally failed. The American government, forced by public opinion, was at last sending an exploratory mission to Brazzaville and the Free French, as the probable first step to providing their desperately needed equipment and arms.

The drowsy little capital was all agog over their coming; this was the event which had been the nightly burden of our prayers. Proudly Richard took me to see the scarlet-uniformed band of grinning black soldiers he was teaching with some difficulty to play The Star-Spangled Banner. They would meet the boat when the members of the mission arrived at the port of Pointe Noire, where I had encountered the King of Luango and witnessed the magic of his naked sorcerers.

A serious problem had arisen in the forthcoming arrangements after the mission boarded the little jungle train that ran from Pointe Noire to Brazzaville; a second band was needed to play the American anthem again when the delegation descended in state at the little depot in the Free French capital. It was difficult enough to teach one band to play the tune; to train two was impossible. Richard had solved the problem with typical Free French ingenuity. After playing the anthem at the Pointe Noire dock, the black musicians would secretly board another coach of the train carrying the mission, change their scarlet uniforms for the blue and gold uniforms of another Free French regiment, and leaving the train at the Brazzaville depot a split second before the delegation, take up their posts on the platform and start playing The Star-Spangled Banner all over.

General Sicé asked me to wait and help in the ceremonies of welcome. I rejected the idea with horror, for I knew it would be a dreadful psychological blunder. The delegation must arrive in this far-off jungle settlement feeling as I had felt, like Stanley finding Livingstone. If they arrived, only to encounter another American and his wife who had come there months before, everything would be ruined.

I discussed in detail with General Sicé some of the

things I would say in London, and set out next day for Lagos, the capital of Nigeria, where we were to change planes for England.

We arrived toward sunset in the humid Nigerian metropolis, where proud Haussas garbed all in white strode up and down the drab main street, and went off for the night to a dismal hotel, though it was the best Lagos afforded. We had been in our room only a moment when a violent thunderstorm began, like that on our first night in Africa. Immediately after, as though it were a signal, a parade of giant cockroaches began, so huge that for an instant my travel-weary eyes took them for rats. I was too well acquainted with these jungle cockroaches to be happy at the sight. There was scarcely a suit or dress in our valises which was not marred with holes, the result of their greedy jaws. These creatures at Lagos seemed even worse; I am sure I could have heard these Lagos roaches eating.

By a black boy I sent a letter to Miles Clifford, the astute and daring Colonial Secretary for Nigeria, who working hand in hand with General Sicé and Le Clerc, had been the chief British conspirator in the plot that had swung the adjoining Vichy colonies to the side of the Allies. He came to the hotel to find us soon after, just as a new invading army of cockroaches was passing in review across the floor.

Our visitor eyed them with horror. "You can't stay in this dreadful place," he declared. "Come out to my house and stay with us."

With joy we let the roaches have the victory, and drove to the Cliffords' beautiful Colonial house in the fashionable suburb of the capital. We were to stay one night, until the arrival of our plane next day for London.

But alas, we became The Man Who Stayed To Dinner.

The one night became two, the two nights became a week. Still we stayed on in the Clifford home, with no sign of when we ever would be leaving. Because of the enemy's hold on the northern routes the flight to England was attended with immense difficulty; only one small plane could get through at rare intervals. On this plane, I was informed, the British military establishment had never carried a woman. Alice or no Alice, no matter how urgent the reason they would not carry a woman now.

The week at the Cliffords' lengthened into another, while my English and Free French friends in Beirut and Cairo and Brazzaville kept the telegraph busy trying to persuade the stern bureau charged with the planes' dispatch to alter its stand against all femininity. Miles Clifford, better known to me now as Geoffrey, added his importunities to the others. Because of our enforced stay in his home it was likely we would have become bitter enemies. But the nephew of Teniel, the illustrator of Alice in Wonderland, he was an individual of deeply artistic tastes. We became devoted friends.

Day after day we waited, living the life of a British colonial novel, going occasionally to the house of the Governor, Sir Bourdillion, for lunch or tea with all the

243

formality and traditions that were the glory of the Empire. Part of the time the Governor was away, and Geoffrey became the acting governor. I watched fascinated the procession of British officials that came to the house, the Attorney-Generals, the Treasurers, and the heavy braided Admirals. On Tuesday nights we would go to the shabby outdoor cinema, and filing in like worshipers in a High Anglican church, take our seats with strict protocol on splintery wooden benches. There we would sit, watching some scratchy film ten or fifteen years old, while malignant mosquitoes chewed our tortured legs, until the story ended. We would rise from our seats and file out again in solemn procession.

Our situation was becoming desperate. We could not stay on abusing the generous hospitality of the Cliffords forever. Even the Man Who Came To Dinner must leave sometime. And I did not feel I could go to London and leave Alice alone in the fever ridden spot that was Lagos in those days. The vivacious Mrs. Clifford had herself been very ill. I knew that Alice would almost certainly not survive.

Again and again I discussed the problem with Geoffrey while more violent Lagos storms thundered and ended, and we came at last to a decision. There was an American steamship line running freighters to the United States at monthly intervals. A boat, the *West Kebar*, was leaving Lagos in a day or two. Alice and I would take the boat to New York and I would go to Washington and tell what

I knew to Lord Halifax, the British Ambassador. From New York transportation to London was comparatively easy. If necessary, after my conference with Halifax, I would fly from New York on the Clipper again and make my report to the Morton Committee and Churchill in person.

We boarded the West Kebar at her dock and steamed slowly down the harbor. The rigging of several freighters sunk by German submarines showed above the water, grim preludes to our voyage. We moved noiselessly out to sea.

As we glided into the blue water, I had no idea how this voyage might end. From British Intelligence I had learned that a German raider was nearby, and within the last few days four British boats had gone to the bottom. Each day America was drawing closer to the war; there were rumors that some ships flying the United States flag had been sunk as well. My English friends in Cairo had given me some very important diplomatic mail for delivery in London, possessing Heaven knew what vital secrets, and Geoffrey had added more letters to my store. Whether the mail or ourselves would ever reach New York was a highly debatable question.

The vessel began a steady roll as we steamed out of sight of land, and I strolled about on my usual tour of investigation. She was a small boat, the West Kebar, known to her crew as the Whiskey Bar, only 3,000 tons, with a tiny deck space seeming scarcely larger than a hotel room between her booms, not a reassuring craft to a bad sailor in which to make a voyage of thousands of miles across the South and North Atlantic. There were four other passengers, American missionaries of some strange religious sect of which I had never heard, who had been improving the lives of the natives in the Congo. Their pale, fanatic faces did not prophesy they would be gay and stimulating companions.

I went up on the bridge for a visit with the Captain, a rigid Vermonter who might have been carved from a block of stone quarried from his native Green Mountains. When he spoke his laconic syllables now and then, his Vermont accent was so pronounced I could comprehend perhaps one word in three. I was compelled to guess the meaning of the others.

I came down to the minute deck again and saw that my gloomy forebodings about the other passengers were only too well founded. They were gathered near the railing with mournful faces, praying dolefully. "O Lord of Hosts. Do not let them sink the ship," they pleaded, over and over.

For several days we steamed in and out of the fever ridden towns that lay along the coast, picking up cargoes of manganese and green-spotted logs of mahogany. Reports came over the air of new ships being sunk; the German raider. disguised as a freighter, was daily growing bolder. Then one afternoon there came the somber word that she had torpedoed another boat, now only a few miles away. The prayers of the missionaries rose to a fever. All day they chanted and pleaded, and far into the night. Their mournful supplications became a sound which the ear soon accepted as a usual accompaniment, like the steady throbbing of the engine or the dull beating of the tom-toms in the jungle.

We were still close to the unseen shore, but the ocean grew empty. Hour by hour we watched the lonely horizon, hoping to see a ship to break the blue monotony. But no vessel ever came into view. The ships were like nervous animals now, daring to move only in packs from the tenuous safety of their harbors. Across the Gulf of Guinea we continued, past the Ivory Coast, and Liberia, and Sierra Leone, while great sea birds flew over us, uttering strange cries, and schools of porpoise danced gracefully before the bow.

On the map Dakar showed ahead, still the stronghold of Vichy, as when we had passed on the Lourenço Marques, and Madame De Larminat had asked me not to send the telegram. I had heard in Lagos that the situation had grown even worse; Vichy airplanes using Dakar as a base now were spotting Allied ships and sending their exact location to the Germans, an act almost certain to be their death warrant.

We began taking a zigzag course to throw off any submarine which might be following, in case a German commander might forget we were an American boat and still officially neutral.

We were almost directly abreast of Dakar, when suddenly a bluish dot appeared where the water met the sky in the direction of the Vichy stronghold. The dot quickly grew larger, soon becoming a reconnaisance plane, painted blue, with every marking carefully painted out so there could be no chance of identification. Warily it flew about us for perhaps a quarter of an hour, as though to learn if we were armed and lure us into firing, then suddenly swooped, and dropping a smoke bomb on our bow, disappeared into the horizon.

The crew of the ship were American merchant seamen unfamiliar so far with the war. Worried when the plane was overhead, they were relieved when it vanished. But my concern was only heightened. I was sure the smoke bomb was the beginning, not the end, of an episode, a signal to someone off in the distance that in a short time was certain to have direct consequences.

We had not long to wait. In perhaps twenty minutes a boat appearing to be a freighter but flying no flag came racing out of the hazy distance. Quickly she slackened speed as she came near, and began steaming around us in an ever-narrowing circle, much as a leopard on the savannas of the nearby shore might circle a gazelle before the final spring.

Still wearing my British uniform, I mentally prepared for a German prison camp. I remembered my mail, and hurrying off to our cabin, picked up a loose piece of iron pipe I had noticed there, and tied it carefully to my bundle of long envelopes that bore the always enigmatic phrase, "On His Majesty's Service." I hurried out to the deck again, and standing at the rail, made ready to throw the bundle overboard.

Nearer and nearer the ship steamed around us, drawing the noose ever tighter and tighter. Then suddenly the whole vessel seemed to come apart, as at the touch of a giant spring. The decks seemed to collapse and the steel sides everywhere swung open. The innocent portholes of a freighter gave way to row on row of cannon, ready to blow us out of the sea. I gave myself and Alice up for lost. With a sinking heart I saw a flag running swiftly up the mast; then with joy as it unfurled I caught a flash of blue stars on white. It was not the swastika of the Nazis; it was a British Q-boat, searching for the German raider.

Swiftly the vessel swept down upon us until she was almost alongside. I could plainly see her stocky British commander, standing at the rail with a megaphone.

"What ship is that?" he bellowed, like the roar of a lion off in the plains.

"West Kebar," called our Captain in the tart accents of Vermont.

The commander of the other boat was not satisfied. "Where were you the night of October 10th?" he bellowed again, somewhat in the manner of the State prosecutor trying a man for murder.

I knew the question was asked in the same way a

banker opening a new account requests the name of the client's mother. If a doubt arises in the future the depositor is again asked the same question; if he fails to respond correctly, he brands himself instantly as a convicted criminal.

This time the other captain was content. The steel sides closed up again like the walls and lid of a jack-in-the-box. The Q-boat steamed away.

Day after day we crawled across the limitless ocean, leaving a dull white wake behind us, like a giant snail. We steamed into the Saragossa Sea, with its vast floating islands of vegetation, stretching across the water like melancholy green mirages. The weather appropriately was stifling, oppressive, without a breath of wind. I thought of all the legends of the men becalmed here in the old days of the sailing ships, and hoped to see an ancient wreck that might have housed some Ancient Mariner.

We steamed beyond the stagnant water once more, into a rolling ocean. A fierce storm assailed us with waves so high they inundated the deck which led to the tiny dining room. A huge sailor picked up Alice and carried her in his arms across the flood as if she were a doll.

All the while the missionaries chanted despairingly, "We are your children, Lord. Spare us, Lord of Hosts."

Then suddenly a few lonely sea gulls drifted overhead, followed soon by battalions and regiments of gulls, squeaking and mewing clamorously, a vast gull army. A hazy shoreline appeared in the distance, then the snow-white top of a solitary skyscraper, as though it were part of an ivory miniature broken off by the Chinese artist who was its creator, and set on the horizon by itself for no good reason. A moment later a vessel swung alongside, and I heard my name shouted and a cheerful insult. It was the police boat bringing the usual photographers and reporters that met the ships before they entered the channel. I saw some newspaper friends at the rail, and heard more raucous salutes. We were back in New York, after ten months abroad and 37 days at sea.

The Ambassador without Portfolio had returned.

We spent a few dazed days in the whirl of Manhattan, gradually becoming accustomed once more to the hot breath of passing busses and the deafening rattle of subways, the throaty murmur of patrician voices from the upper East Side and the comic accents of Brooklyn. I sent on my letters to Lord Halifax in Washington and received word he would like me to come down to lunch the following Friday. But something unusual occurred the intervening Sunday—something known to history as Pearl Harbor. On the frenzied Monday which followed I communicated with the Embassy, certain that Lord Halifax would wish to cancel the appointment. To my surprise, he sent a message saying that he wanted me to come nevertheless. The matter, involving as it did the entire relationship between the British and the Free French, he felt was too important to permit any delay.

I took the train to Washington, and with the small-town Kentucky tradition of promptness, arrived at the British Embassy on the stroke of twelve, the hour of the appointment.

Lord Halifax hurried in ten minutes late, breathless with apology. "I'm terribly sorry I'm late," he said. "But Roosevelt wouldn't let me get away from the White House."

I couldn't help smiling inwardly. The Ambassador wasn't doing too badly, after all.

We had lunch and after lunch a long talk. I had been strongly prejudiced against Halifax by what I had read before our meeting, the part he had played in the Munich appeasement, his difficult, frigid personality. After a few moments of conversation my prejudices disappeared. Much of what were considered his stiffness and coldness I am sure was an almost paralyzing shyness. I told him all I had observed in Africa and Syria and how I believed the situation could be remedied. He asked me to put the report in writing so he could forward it to London.

I wrote the report with my recommendations a short time later, a repetition of what I had already told my friends in Damascus and Beirut and Cairo. I urged again that certain definite steps be taken to restore the old cordiality between the two once closely-knit Allies. What I wrote took no particular intelligence. Any mildly observant newspaper man would have been forced to the same conclusions. The report recommended, among other things, that both the British and the Free French start campaigns among their troops to destroy the false legend that British and French could not live in harmony. It recommended that the Free French movement be given a firm base, a kind of charter to eliminate the criticism I had heard so often in Syria, "Why should we respect this government? This is no government. This is only one man." It recommended that outstanding Free Frenchmen like General Sicé be brought to America and perhaps England to lessen the dependence on General De Gaulle, and let the world see for itself the quality of the men who had created the Free French rebellion.

I was happy when I learned later that almost all my recommendations became part of the Allied plan, and felt my labors hadn't been in vain.

There isn't much more to tell. I had only been back a few weeks when I found I couldn't end my advocacy of the Free French cause as I had hopefully expected. The State Department, though forced to help the rebels at Brazzaville, in actuality was bitterly hostile to the movement and to me personally as well. Their Ambassador hadn't reported what they wanted to hear. I could tell of the harsh pressures brought to bear to make me stop writing, pressures so intense that I finally laid the situation before my old friend Elmer Davis, director of the Office of War Information, and told him if the pressures did not stop, I would reluctantly be forced to make the whole affair public, with a disastrous effect on the morale of all authors supposed to be making the world safe for freedom. The pressures ended overnight. I could tell—

But let these episodes lie buried and forgotten. Like an old lion, only a toothless old dog too weary to hunt digs up ancient bones.

There were amusing moments afterward, such as the time when General Sicé, in New York on his way to London, and seeing Potage Vichysoisse on the Algonquin menu, smilingly asked if that was the way I treated an old Free French friend I had invited to lunch. The smile deepened when Frank Case, then the Algonquin owner, took a pencil and changed the offending soup to "Potage De Gaulle, nee Vichyssoisse," the way it read for a long time after.

There were exciting moments when I later wrote some vitriolic columns for the editorial page of the New York Herald Tribune about the Men of Vichy and the Darlan Deal and had the pleasure of seeing words destroy a corrupt enemy as effectively as a bullet.

There was a highly emotional moment in those tense days while I was attacking Darlan, when Adrien Tixier, the representative of the Free French in America asked me to come to his office, and with tears in his eyes, thanked me in the name of the French people for what I had done in the past and was doing now.

And there was that final delicious moment of triumph, when the Free French were officially recognized by

America as Allies, and I could have said, "I told you so," but discreetly didn't.

I met De Gaulle again a few years later. He had mellowed considerably. There was a graciousness in his manner lacking in the De Gaulle of Brazzaville. There is little superficial resemblance between the lean, bitter De Gaulle of those days and the somewhat paunchy figure, smilingly shaking hands with premiers and kings today at the Presidential Palace in Paris. Yet it is obvious that much of the earlier character survives, and explains many of his actions that might otherwise seem difficult to understand. And one fact any nation or any individual dealing with De Gaulle or any Frenchman of his generation will do well to remember: The defeat of the French army by the Germans was a blow to the fierce French pride impossible to comprehend by any except those who witnessed the tragedy. The French were left with a sense of inferiority and humiliation which unconsciously they will spend the rest of their lives trying to erase.

I sit at my desk, and I think of the men I knew in those far-off days that now seem like a fantastic novel. Leclerc and General Sicé are dead, Leclerc a hero revered by his countrymen; Sicé, to whom the French owe even more, completely forgotten. Almost every day I see pictures of De Gaulle, chief of state, discussing world affairs with ministers and parliaments, or, ironically, receiving the salute of a trim honor guard of the German Army. But I see him better as the gaunt figure followed by the forlorn dog as he reviewed the pathetic Free French troops or when he offered me one of my own cigarettes in my white-verandaed house on the Congo.

In England Brian Guinness is now Lord Moyne and Air Commodore Buss is in the Foreign Office, his exploits forever hidden within some musty storehouse in the secret files of the Crown. Geoffrey, director of the Lord Leverhulme Foundation and one of his country's most distinguished citizens, is now Sir Miles Clifford, knighted for his valiant services in Africa by the Queen. It is to his cheerful home in Hampstead with his lovely wife and family that I first make my way on my rare visits to London. But I see him best at the hotel in Lagos, rescuing us from the giant cockroaches and making us The Man Who Came To Dinner.

I think of the Clipper that took us to Lisbon and Monsieur X and the Lourenço Marques and the telegram that was never sent and the blue ocean off Dakar. I think of the children with the parrots on their arm and the hotel where the jackals raced past our beds and the Portuguese boatman with the great earrings, like a pirate in his prime. I think of Brazzaville and the witch doctors of Luango and the steamboats, sending out showers of sparks from their stacks as they ploughed through the endless jungle. I think of the monkeys and the tsetse flies and the cannibals and the kindly King of the Pygmies. I think of Bangui and the wild dogs and Bouca and the elders in their leopard skins and the child who was a lukundu. I think of Fort Lamy and the black sultan in the beehive hut and the camel troops near Mao. And I think of Cairo and our occupation of Beirut and the beautiful Druse princess in the Hollywood bungalow complete with Hollywood bar.

And then I carefully study my faded documents, the copies of my cables and dispatches and my passes for the Front and my secret maps given me by Leclerc. And I look at my grim ju ju on the mantel and my Congo death mask and my throwing knife that cuts anywhere it touches and my graceful bow as tall as a man, and my quiver of poison arrows.

For this is the only way that I know the story is true and that all of these fantastic events really happened. This is the only way I can tell it is not a manuscript found in a bottle.

THE END

PAPERS FOUND
IN A BUREAU DRAWER

WORLD SCOOP

New York World-Telegram

Copyright, 1941 by New York World-Telegram Corporation. All rights reserved.

Local Forecast: Partly cloudy, not much change in temperature; warmer and probably fair Sunday.

VOL. 73.—NO. 258.—IN TWO SECTIONS—SECTION ONE   NEW YORK, FRIDAY, MAY 2, 1941.   A

NIGH

Latest Wall St. Pri

PRICE THREE CEN

FREE FRENCH RALLY IN AFRICA
AS COLONIES FACE INVASIO

Nazi 'Chutists Died Like Flies

By RICHARD D. McMILLAN and HENRY T. GORRELL,
United Press Staff Correspondents

WITH THE BRITISH EMPIRE TROOPS EVACUATED FROM GREECE, CAIRO, May 2—Back in Egypt after a terrible 300-mile retreat through Greece and a 600-mile voyage across the sea under the attack of German dive bombers, the undaunted British Imperial Expeditionary Force began today to reorganize for another fight.

Its men had fought the massed armored forces of the Germans for days, they had fired until their ammunition gave out at robot-like waves of massed German infantrymen, who marched endlessly over the bodies of their own dead until the attackers were exhausted.

They had fought parachutists who had descended by thousands in an attempt to cut off their final retreat.

They had embarked on the beaches of the Peloponnesus, had made the voyage across the eastern Mediterranean, and had been crowded into overloaded evacuation ships, singing

below decks as the gun crews above fought a final furious—and successful—fight with the Stuka bombers.

Hundreds of soldiers, crowded on the docks because there was no room below, cheered as the gunners of the three antiaircraft cruisers nearest us blazed at German and Italian planes.

Just before we reached port a military funeral was held for one man who had been wounded by a bomb fragment before he embarked and died aboard our ship. The transport came to a dead stop as his body was lowered into the sea and 12 riflemen fired a salute.

The British Expeditionary Force, its tank men without tanks, its aviators without planes, its exhausted artillerymen without guns, its infantrymen and machine gunners, its nurses and surgeons tirelessly tending the wounded, and with the Greek and Yugoslav stragglers who escaped with us had not only a story to tell of disaster but also of heroism.

With us also were women and children, the youngest

child 10 months old, and one American woman who had escaped from Yugoslavia and joined the British army at an island she reached with her Canadian husband. A New Yorker, her father is a United States Treasury representative at Toronto.

The British Expeditionary Force had fought day and night up to the beaches of the Peloponnesus where the German parachutists machine-gunned the small boats which put out from the shore.

And on the voyage to Egypt the surgeons and nurses fought a fight with death in treating the wounded.

It was necessary to leave some of the wounded behind, in charge of a base hospital corps which volunteered to remain with them.

But as for the Expeditionary Force proper, an Australian brigadier said aboard our transport:

"All but the damned fools, the stragglers and the unfortunates wounded or killed along the roads, by the

(Continued on Page Thirteen.)

Army Sworn To Redeem Homeland

Youth from Many Parts Of World Join De Gaulle In 'Valley Forge' Stand

By BEN LUCIEN BURMAN
NEA Service Staff Correspondent.

BRAZZAVILLE, French Equatorial Africa, (by Mail)—There have been many mysteries in this many riddles to which even the most astute diplomats could possess the solution. But perhaps the one of which, more than any other, has occupied the attention of Americans is this:

Is defeated France dead beyond hope of resurrection? To find the answer to that question I have to deep into the tangled jungles which Stanley and shame opened to the white man in the last century, I think I can give the answer.

Truly, the heart of France is no longer to beyond the gentle Seine. It is here in De Gaulle Africa, also banks of the fever-ridden Congo.

A few kilometres from where I am writing this patch the towering equatorial forests begin—with elephants and gorillas and great green pythons.

The dread insects fly everywhere beyond the jungs, for this is the heart of the sleeping sickness and the small settlement's population 250 contracted awful malaria last year.

The great armies of African ants—black and re a ghostly gray—are constantly killing night and the But there is another army marching in here army sworn to drive the Germans from France.

Every day new recruits to this army are rush sometimes by boat, sometimes by canoe, sometim tramping for weeks and months through the swarm

Strike Halts Ferry Line

8 Vessels Tied Up As 100 Walk Out

Dumbfounded by negotiations over wage controversies and working conditions more than 100 employees—crew members and terminal workers of the Electric Ferries, Inc. went on strike at midnight last night, holding service to the Jersey Shore of the line.

Boats tied up at their piers include four that ply between the St. Brooklyn, and St. George, S I., one that runs between Perth Richmond, S. I., and Bayonne, N. J. and three which operate between W. 23d St., Manhattan, and Weehawken, N. J.

No attempt will be made to operate the line during the strike according to Clarence D. Walker

Orders 7-Day Week on Defense

EXTRA!

By the United Press.

WASHINGTON, May 2—President Roosevelt, asserting that America is confronted by a "critical situation," ordered the Office of Production Management today to put operations of defense machines and machine tools on a 54-hour day, seven-day week.

In a letter to William S. Knudsen and Sidney Hillman, directors of OPM, Mr. Roosevelt requested a "triple program."

Pool every useful or potentially useful machine tool and machine in the country for use in the defense program.

Utilize these machines and tools where they are, or transport them to a point where they can be useful.

Herntoviase the entire nation, including the armed forces, for skilled workers to operate the machines on an all-out basis.

Fight Transfer Of Axis Ships

Some Senators See It as 'Act of War'

BY LONDON.

BERLIN, May 1—The American threat to the European question raised "disunity describ the interests of property attend'em to the question of seni-official text.
Dentschland commentary arose in the Wilhelmstrasse by the marine Germans assailed adhered this period first. "Scrap has the Reich pursued any other policy in the Western Hemisphere than that of leghone commercial objectives." Herren added, "There are no grounds for trouble between two peoples

Hitler Coveting French Morocco

Petain Beset by Axis Pressure, Disloyalty at Home and Hunger

By WILLIAM PHILIP SIMMS,
Scripps-Howard Foreign Editor.

WASHINGTON, May 2—Sorely beset France and her French Empire in Africa and Asia today face a new threat of invasion.

Military sources in London are quoted here as saying a grand-scale drive against Suez and Gibraltar may start within the next week or 10 days. Meanwhile Hitler is threatening to occupy Free France and her African colonies—including the island of Madagascar—and Japan is reported to be all set to seize Indo-China.

Hitler has long coveted French Morocco. With French and Spanish Morocco in his hands he would be able to close

U. S. Arms Reach

New York World-Telegram

e Gaulle 'Exposes' Petain as Advocate
f Surrender Long Before Armistice

*neral de Gaulle, gaunt and angular "Jean d'Arc" of Free
whose words and movements have been veiled in secrecy
e elected a year ago to carry on from distant shores his
's war against Germany, has broken his silence in a revela-
terview with Ben Lucien Burman, distinguished American
t. Burman is now in the de Gaulle-controlled area of French
The following dispatch, written immediately after Burman's
w with General de Gaulle earlier in the month, has just
ceived in America by wireless.*

By BEN LUCIEN BURMAN.
Copyright, 1941, NEA Service, Inc.

AZZAVILLE, French West Africa, June 18.—From
ngle heart of Africa, General Charles de Gaulle
s today that Marshal Petain was beaten even before
k supreme command of the retreating French army
8 of last year.

ance is done; we must surrender!" T'
eral de Gaulle, was the aged Petain
remier Reynaud nearly a full mo
-German armistice.
s revelation was made in an ex

NEW YORK
Herald Tribune

"The Vichy Men of Africa"

APPEASEMENT is always the blood
brother of cowardice; appease-
'nt of Vichy is folly as well.
Last spring I was traveling through
the Congo, gloomy land of
poison and fever. In B-
capital, and the
in the black
with hu-
ine-

By Ben Lucien Burman

edly different. "The Germans have
spread their tentacles everywhere,"
he said. "It has not been invasion.
It has been something far subtler.
The morale of the people has been
undermined, shattered. They are
tired, discouraged. The Free French
leaders—any one who openly dared
show his sympathies—have all been
removed from office and put in
son. All the chiefs now are out-
out Vichy men—collaboration-

the philosophical differences between totalitarianism and democracy, the rights and wrongs of Vichy
and Free France. He fights the
man his captain. Thus the change of
the enemy. He points out a
hundred key officers can change
the course of an African war.
It is a relief to turn from the
contemplation of the sorry men of
Vichy to the heroic figures of the
Free French in Africa. With General de Gaulle and his fellows of
the newly created Free French government in London and Generals
Catroux and De Larminat and the
others in far-off Syria, they are to
be numbered among those few
human beings in that rarest half
of fame: men who have sacrificed
appiness, family, life itself for the
e of an ideal.

ll they still fight if the Ger-
ce grew gloomy. "Many of
ice as invaders?"
ans and some of the young-
would. The rest of the
stion. The older officers
nd-picked for Vichy and
The black troops fol-

utstanding among the leaders in
ca are General Le Claire, the
aristocrat captor of Kufra, a French
that gave Lafayette to the type
with the only word in his Ameri-
vocabulary "forward," who
figure, who, though
rank or gene-
his life in

American author visits the heart of Africa,
Frenchmen of all classes are joining De Gaulle,
to battle Hitler, to found a new France

Free France on Le Congo

Condensed from

The Reader's Digest

Ben Lucien Burm

N THE palm-fringed river
Negroes glide past in a dugout, chanting as they ply
long paddles. On the shore
en in fantastic costumes
talking in their curious
d language that rushes
a waterfall. Deep in the
st I hear the throbbing
tomtom, beating out its
sterious message. This is
Congo, heart of the darkness
Africa.
Suddenly the sharp beat of mili-
y drums drowns the far-off throb-
g. Troops march past, white
ldiers with gay young faces, sing-
g Madelon. An airplane marked
ith the cross of Lorraine appears

overhead. Here, a
France miraculously s
In Paris the spirit of H
entombed beneath the swastika.
Vichy the old men join
hands with their conquerors.
Here in Brazzaville, capital
of De Gaulle's Free France,
brave men are rallying and
taking oath never to return
to their native land so long
as a single German soldier stands
on its soil.
It is stirring, it is moving — and
important. De Gaulle Africa is a
vast empire, stretching from the
busy Atlantic ports of Pointe Noire
and Douala 2000 miles across forest
and desert to Egypt. It controls the
Tchad, keystone of an arch formed
by the British colonies fringing both
coasts of the continent. Should this
keystone fall the Nazis could push
down between the two pillars of
British territory and take the heart
of the continent. The Belgians
frankly admit that but for the
Free French their colony just across
the Congo River would long ago
have been seized by the Germans,
covetous of its rubber and metals.
Moreover, the Tchad, with its

A FEW OF

THE MANY

HEADLINES

THE FIRST DISPATCH

BRAZZAVILLE VIA LEOPOLDVILLE
FRENCH CONGO
APRIL 19, 1941

PRESSE COLLECT
NENPRISE NEW YORK

FRED* DON** URGE DO EVERYTHING POSSIBLE HELP THESE PEOPLE GET REC-
OGNITION ARMS US PERHAPS NEA OR SCRIPPS HOWARD CAMPAIGN OR ANY
OTHER WAY · CAN BE ENORMOUS FACTOR WINNING WAR STOP · HAVE
SWELL INSIDE STUFF PRESENT SITUATION DAKAR MOROCCO WEYGAND PETAIN

BEGIN STORY

THERE HAVE BEEN MANY MYSTERIES THIS WAR MANY RIDDLES TO WHICH
EVEN MOST ASTUTE DIPLOMAT DOES NOT POSSESS SOLUTION · BUT PERHAPS
ONE QUESTION MORE THAN ANY OTHER HAS OCCUPIED MINDS AMERICANS ·
IS DEFEATED FRANCE DEAD BEYOND HOPE RESURRECTION

TO FIND ANSWER THAT QUESTION I HAVE TRAVELED DEEP INTO TANGLED
JUNGLES WHICH STANLEY AND LIVINGSTON OPENED TO WHITE MAN IN LAST
CENTURY · AND THINK CAN ANSWER THAT QUESTION TRULY · HEART OF
FRANCE NO LONGER IN PARIS ALONG GENTLE SEINE · IT IS HERE IN DE
GAULLE AFRICA ALONG BANKS OF FEVER RIDDEN CONGO

FEW KILOMETERS FROM WHERE AM WRITING THIS DISPATCH TOWERING
EQUATORIAL FORESTS BEGIN WITH THEIR ELEPHANTS AND GORILLAS AND
GREEN PYTHONS · DREAD TSTSE FLY IS EVERYWHERE BEYOND CLEARINGS FOR
THIS IS HEART SLEEPING SICKNESS AREA AND OF THIS SMALL SETTLEMENT'S
POPULATION LAST YEAR TWO HUNDRED AND TWENTY CONTRACTED MALADY ·
THE GREAT ARMIES AFRICAN ANTS BLACK AND RED AND A GHOSTLY GRAY
ARE TOILING CONSTANTLY NIGHT AND DAY

BUT THERE IS ANOTHER ARMY TOILING CEASELESSLY ARMY SWORN DRIVE
GERMANS FROM FRANCE · EVERY DAY THEY ARE ARRIVING SOMETIMES BY
BOAT SOMETIMES BY CANOE SOMETIMES BY TRAMPING FOR WEEKS AND
MONTHS THROUGH THE SWAMPS AND FORESTS · FROM FRANCE FROM TIBET
FROM INDO CHINA FROM DAKAR THEY MAKE THEIR WAY TO THIS SWELTER-
ING OUTPOST SCIENTISTS AND STUDENTS GENERALS AND PRIESTS PEASANTS
AND SIMPLE SOLDIERS · CATHOLICS PROTESTANTS JEWS GUIDED ONLY BY AN
IDEAL AND DEVOTION TO CAUSE OF THEIR LEADER GENERAL DE GAULLE

* *Fred Ferguson, President, NEA Service (Scripps Howard)*
** *Don Sutton, Executive Editor, NEA Service (Scripps Howard)*

A SHORT DISTANCE BEYOND MY WINDOW IN THE NEWLY ERECTED CAMP
D'ORNANO HELMETED YOUNG FRENCHMEN FROM ALL OVER THE WORLD ARE
DRILLING IN THE FIERY SUN TO GIVE DEFIANCE TO PETAIN WHO SAID IT WAS
THE YOUTH OF FRANCE WHO HAD FAILED THEIR COUNTRY · "IT WAS NOT THE
YOUTH OF FRANCE" THEY TELL ME "IT WAS PETAIN AND THE OTHER WEAK
OLD MEN WHO FAILED US AND BETRAYED US"

IT WAS AN IRONIC TRICK OF FATE THAT FIRST TO RALLY TO DE GAULLE'S
APPEAL TO DISOBEY ARMISTICE SHOULD BE FEW FRENCH PATRIOTS IN THIS
REMOTE FEVER RIDDEN REGION SO LONG KNOWN AS WHITE MAN'S GRAVE-
YARD · BUT IT WAS LUCKY FATE · FOR AREA THEY CONTROL IS IMMENSE REACH-
ING FROM THE ATLANTIC 2000 MILES ACROSS THE HEART OF AFRICA TO
ANGLO EGYPTIAN FRONTIER · IT POSSESSES STRATEGIC VALUE WHICH CAN-
NOT BE ESTIMATED · FREE FRENCH HOLD TCHAD · AND IS MILITARY AXIOM
HERE THEY WHO HOLD TCHAD HOLD AFRICA · TCHAD IS KEY LINK THAT JOINS
BRITISH COLONIES OF EAST COAST WITH COLONIES ON WEST · WITHOUT AID
OF FREE FRENCH ALMOST EVERY BRITISH COLONY IN AFRICA WOULD TODAY
BE IN PERIL AND HUGE PART AFRICA WITH IMMENSE WAR RESOURCES MIGHT
BE IN POSSESSION OF GERMANS

THE AMBASSADOR SENDS A CABLE

AMBASSADOR BIDDLE   AMERICAN EMBASSY   LONDON

AS YOU REQUESTED HAVE MADE CLOSE STUDY OF DE GAULLE MOVEMENT
AND OFFICIALS HERE · REPRESENT FINEST OF FRENCH · MAGNIFICENT SPIRIT
YOUNG AND OLD LIKE EARLY AMERICAN PATRIOTS · REPRESENT EVERY QUALITY
CHERISHED BY AMERICANS · COMING HERE EVERY DAY SCIENTISTS STUDENTS
GENERALS LABOR LEADERS PRIESTS SURMOUNTING TERRIFIC DIFFICULTIES
MANY DYING IN ATTEMPT TO FIGHT GERMANY · THINK OF ENORMOUS IMPOR-
TANCE IF IMPOSSIBLE FULL RECOGNITION FORMULA BE WORKED OUT SOME
KIND OF RECOGNITION BE GIVEN THEM LIKE BRITISH · AND URGE PLANES AND
ARMS BE SENT · WAITING AND EAGER TO FIGHT BUT LACK MATERIALS · URGE
AND URGE AGAIN SEND THEM SOMETHING · NEED NOT BE SUPPLIES VAST
QUANTITIES THAT WOULD WEAKEN BRITISH EFFORT BUT MERELY ENOUGH TO
EQUIP SOME TROOPS HERE AND KEEP UP MORALE THESE TRULY HEROIC FIG-
URES AND LET THEM FEEL NOT DESERTED BY UNITED STATES · CAN BE ENOR-
MOUS FACTOR IN SAVING FRANCE AND RESTORING HER TO SELF RESPECT
AND POTENTIAL WAR CONTRIBUTION · IMPORTANCE OF MOVEMENT AND
GREAT STRATEGIC AID PROSECUTION AFRICAN AND MEDITERRANEAN CAM-
PAIGNS . . .

REPORT TO HALIFAX

A Letter to Lord Halifax, British Ambassador to the U. S.

New York
December Twenty-Sixth, 1941

Dear Lord Halifax:

I am so sorry that an extremely vigorous African reaction combined with a long delayed surgical patching up made necessary by the last war prevented me until now from putting down my conclusions about those matters which I had the pleasure of discussing with you in Washington.

Before I set these down, with a view toward future harmonious relations between the British and the Free French it might be well to say that I think the British should be prepared to admit to themselves that the original mistake that led to the deterioration of their relations last summer was on the British side, and have thus a charitable view in understanding what followed. I mention this because there are certain important Englishmen I have met who are rather inclined to dismiss the Free French as a group of hysterical individuals whose chief quality is ingratitude. Through a series of extraordinary coincidences and my friendships with figures on both sides, I had an unusual opportunity of watching the entire situation as it developed. Of all I observed one fact emerges clearly: The Syrian armistice terms were a serious blunder; the mistakes of the Free French followed as a consequence, and were the natural results of the inferior position in which they had been placed by the document of Acre.

But it is remedies, not history, with which this letter is concerned. So, entirely for what they may be worth, as you requested, here are those ideas which occurred to me in Syria when I was in the midst of the crisis there, and later. Some of these matters I have already discussed with British officers and diplomatic officials in Africa and the Middle East; at the risk of being repetitious I will put them down here with the others.

One. There should be a definite press and propaganda campaign on the part of the British among their troops in the Middle East to inspire them with confidence in the Free French movement, and in Free Frenchmen. On arriving in Cairo . . . from French Equatorial Africa where relations between the British and the Free French were superb, I was instantly struck by the suspicious attitude of the British troops toward their Free French colleagues. The stories I heard of Free French deceptiveness and treachery were so venomous and followed such similar patterns, that I am convinced they were directed by enemy propaganda agents seeking to create a division between these two allies. I could cite you numerous examples. The same thing occurred in Syria, that other glorious breeding ground of intrigue, where enemy propagandists lost no opportunity of furthering the division when it finally developed.

Once the British have launched such a campaign, I think the Free French would be equally wise to institute similar measures with their own troops. The supposed natural antagonism of the Anglo-Saxon and the Latin is a highly fallacious legend, disproved until the Syrian crisis by the close co-operation of the British and French at Brazzaville and Fort Lamy. It is a legend which thrives chiefly by its repetition; if the Allies allow themselves to play the German game by fostering it, I think they are most unwise.

Two. With all the respect that I have for General De Gaulle, with all my appreciation of his accomplishments and sacrifices, I regret to say that I think his name should be kept out of the Free French movement and the publicity connected with it wherever possible. I think any policy which tends to indicate that the movement is a one man, personal affair is extremely dangerous. This would be dangerous with any individual; it is particularly so in the case of De Gaulle, who seems to be a natural trouble maker. I am convinced that the Syrian problem would have been settled with comparative ease had he not been present. He was always inflaming the reasonable men to anger. I know this to my sorrow; as I told you, hour after hour and day after day I labored in Beirut and the suburbs of the Lebanon, trying to pour oil on troubled waters, only to find De Gaulle creating new storms, new crises. I think he must certainly be kept in London, and in a position where he can do no harm. He strikes me as a man of keen talents, but of the ascetic, schoolmaster type, with a decided tendency toward mental arrogance, and an unwillingness to listen to the other person's point of view. I think he would be very difficult at a peace conference. It would seem to me that putting him in some decorative position where he remained a valuable legend, and was not compelled to meet people, would be a good solution of the problem. For whenever he meets other men, he makes enemies. He is enormously unpopular with the British in the Middle East and on the West Coast of Africa, to such an extent that unless there has been a revolutionary change in his character, his usefulness in those areas is unquestionably and irrevocably at an end.

Three. I think it vital that the Free French movement be given a firmer, broader foundation. It was far too vague and nebulous when I mentioned this matter to your officials last summer, and since I left the area the creation of the new Free French ministry in London has probably greatly improved the situation. But it still seems to me to lack the form which helps to give any government stability; it needs some definiteness, some sort of charter. To certain types of mentalities a document of this kind has particular appeal. Let it be a declaration of principles or whatever phrase that may be evolved, and decorate it with a large, impressive gold seal. Call it the Fourth French Republic, or any other name that seems fitting; only it must be a name that gives a feeling of solidity. I am sure this would have an important effect in the colonies. Time after time I have had Syrians and the Druses and even other Frenchmen complain to me: "But why should we respect or obey this government? This is no government. This is only one man."

Four. I think that after such a charter and such a government have been evolved, a careful campaign should be instituted to broaden the entire base of the Free French movement, and to enroll in it every desirable type of Frenchman from all classes and all political creeds. Perhaps with such a reorganized group it might even be possible to obtain certain liberal key figures now in unoccupied France, and if they can be slipped out of the country, have them take part in the movement's direction. . . . Until I left the United States last winter I was chairman of the dinner committee of the American PEN Club, and I have had excellent opportunity of seeing that there are numerous important Frenchmen who are at present outside the Free French movement because they suspect De Gaulle of fascism. I think they would join very quickly a broad organization in which they could have full confidence.

To further this confidence I can think of no better way than to bring to America—and perhaps to England—one or two of the outstanding Free Frenchmen from Africa and let the French in this country with the Americans see that really superb Frenchmen are still on the earth. They are magnificent, the Free French soldiers in Equatorial Africa, officers and men alike. I think it would be enormously helpful if General Sicé, the present High Commissioner there, were brought to London, and to America. He is a truly great man, in my opinion by far the most important figure in the whole movement, and a figure whom I hope after the war will become president of France. Moreover he is a man of immense personal charm, whom everyone worships at first sight; he is the ideal figure needed for a popular movement. To keep him hidden in Africa at a time when men of his sort are so desperately needed to recreate confidence in the French everywhere, seems to me a waste that is appalling.

As I stated in the beginning, I am putting down these suggestions for what they are worth. The hourly developments of the war may make them utterly valueless. If they are of the slightest use, and make the slightest contribution to the information on which you and your government must base your decisions, I shall be deeply grateful.

It was a very great pleasure lunching with you and the charming Lady Halifax. Will you please give her my very best regards? And I hope her nice dog who sat so patiently—and hopefully—beside me is flourishing.

With All Good Wishes For The Holiday Season
And The Coming Year,

Faithfully,

BEN LUCIEN BURMAN

CADDY-BURMAN
SAFARI

THE GENERAL PAYS A CALL

MERCI

REPUBLIQUE FRANÇAISE

ORDRE NATIONAL DE LA LÉGION D'HONNEUR

HONNEUR   PATRIE

M. Ben Lucien *Burman.*

Journaliste

est nommé *Chevalier de la Légion d'Honneur*

pour prendre rang du 23 Septembre 1976

Fait à Paris le 19 Novembre 1976

NIGERIA

Atlantic Ocean

Pointe Noire
San Antonio Do Zai